BERT BRECHT

Modern Literature Monographs

BERT BRECHT

Willy Haas

Translated by
Max Knight and Joseph Fabry

Frederick Ungar Publishing Co.
New York

Published by special arrangement with Colloquium Verlag, Berlin, publishers of the original German *Bert Brecht*.

832.09
H

Contents

1   Prologue: Bert Brecht between
     Two Worlds   1

2   Small and Great Beginnings   13

3   The Threepenny Opera *and its*
     Consequences   47

4   Epilogue *to* The Threepenny Opera   59

5   Theory and Practice of the
     "Didactic Plays"   69

6   Postscript for the Second
     German Edition   105

7   Epilogue: Brecht's Literary
     Estate   109

    Chronology   113

    Selected Bibliography   117

Translators' Note

Translated titles of works by Bertolt Brecht or by other authors mentioned in the book follow the form chosen in published translations (e.g., *Warren Hastings* for *Kalkutta, 4. Mai*); where we did not find a published translation, we supplied our own titles.

All verse, rhymed or unrhymed, are original translations.

The word *Verfremdung*—a special coinage, not identical with *Entfremdung*—means, approximately, "breaking the illusion of the theater audience"; to avoid confusion we followed the tradition, well entrenched in Brecht literature, of rendering it as "alienation," a not very felicitous choice.

The Epilogue was prepared by the author for the American edition.

We wish to acknowledge the research done for this translation by Mr. Anthony C. Knight.

M. K. and J. F.

1

Prologue: Bert Brecht between Two Worlds

To understand Bertolt Brecht's personality it is perhaps best to talk first about his disguises. In the 1920's, the time of Brecht's great successes—*Die Dreigroschenoper (The Threepenny Opera)* and *Hauspostille (Manual of Piety)*—it was easy to spot him in Berlin if one wanted to. He was always fully masqueraded: his costume consisted of an old, dark, close-fitting, well-worn jacket of soft leather like a motorcyclist's or a truck driver's, yet underneath he wore an expensive silk shirt which only men of substantial income could afford. Never missing was the cap favored by the proletarian of 1920 or the football coach of today. His head was usually shaved like a convict's or a basic trainee's. But most curious was a pair of steel-rimmed glasses which could hardly be bought in Berlin any more at that time—the kind a schoolteacher from some provincial town might have worn. When Brecht wished to read, he would carefully take these glasses from their case, clean them, slip them over his ears, and, after the reading, just as carefully replace them in his breast pocket.

It was a costume—but for more than one role. There was a touch of the supersecret commissar from a mysterious Moscow bureau in it, whom popular fancy at that time envisaged in leather jackets; but also a bit of the schoolmaster apt to dictate stylized banalities in a slow, hard voice; and certainly also a touch of the gangster-and-prostitute atmosphere of *The Threepenny Opera, Aufstieg und Fall der Stadt Mahagonny (Rise and Fall of the City Mahagonny*), and his plays using a Chicago gangster background. And there was always the shorn head, the almost lipless hard mouth, the curious stony face that looked like a convict's.

He was a jumble of masks, disguises, calculated gestures, and props, apparently thrown together at random and yet significant. To me his face revealed nothing of the great tenderness of some of his early love and idyllic poetry nor of the magnificent animalistic pantheism of his Panic hymns. He was always disguised, as small boys dress up as Indians; only the touch of the schoolteacher seemed genuine. Yet, women did seem to sense his animalism and found him attractive.

Despite this masquerade his appearance was frightening rather than amusing. I found his self-assured, didactic manner of speaking uncanny because I was unable to discover the depth that might have justified his self-assurance. At that time he was not yet the strict Marxist and dialectic materialist. The Ullstein author Bert Brecht grew very slowly into the Communist Bert Brecht. During that period his theories were vague, emotional, cynical, threatening, icy, and by their sharp, concise formulation promised far more than they delivered. They were primitive yet mysterious.

Soon a critical period was to come. The cynical, gripping power of the songs of *The Threepenny Opera* had swept Berliners off their feet. But then followed a sharp unexpected decline, a crash. Brecht produced *Happy End*, a play so weak that it is not even included in the fourteen volumes of his collected plays. At the Berlin world premiere, *Happy End* could hardly be played to the end because of the hissing, the mocking laughter, and the noisy slamming of doors by the audience that had only yesterday cheered him enthusiastically. It was one of Berlin's worst theater scandals. Oddly enough, Brecht later attributed the authorship of this hapless piece to his faithful assistant Elisabeth Hauptmann who had helped him in this work as in most of his others. He specifically named her as the author of *Happy End* in his *Versuche (Experiments)* No. 13:5, published by Kiepenheuer in 1932, although the play had been performed with his name on the program.

The fate of the opera *Rise and Fall of the City Mahagonny* was not much better in spite of the stirring songs by Kurt Weill. Here, all the primitive, cynical themes—the absolute right of the strong over the weak, the haves over the have-nots, brutality over law, the ridiculous impotence of the spirit when facing the iron fist—that are found in his plays since *Mann ist Mann (A Man's a Man)* and *The Threepenny Opera* are mechanically repeated, belabored to absurdity, and worked to death. It is hard to understand that his intelligent, talented collaborator Peter Suhrkamp had not retained enough objectivity to see this. (He is no longer named as collaborator in the collected works.)

Brecht still had a large following and enjoyed the support of such influential men as the critic

Herbert Ihering. But even the faithful admirers who believed in his future were wondering what was to come.

Like Charles Baudelaire and in some ways Arthur Rimbaud, Brecht was a curious kind of extremist. His creative power drew inspiration from only two extremes: one was a churning, stunning, boundless sensuality, the lasciviousness and the lawlessness of the jungle; the other was a love for whatever was cold, hard, sharp, and deadly—the blade of the executioner, the cold barrel of the revolver, the steel of arm and leg irons (including the dogmatic shackles of the Party), the inquisition, Machiavellianism, and the dictatorship that makes short shrift of its enemies.

Young Bert Brecht would have subscribed to Joseph de Maistre's pronouncement, so admired by Baudelaire: that human society is built upon the institutions of the soldier, the priest, and the hangman. To be sure, Brecht's soldier was the blindly loyal soldier of the Party and the Agitprop; the priest, some shaman of Marxism in one of the inquisition chambers of Stalin's prison; and the hangman, the importance of whom in creating state and society, Brecht never had any doubt about during that period.

Baudelaire was master of his own difficult kind of writing. He was able to contain desire, lasciviousness, jungle drives, and perversity within the steel bands of form—his classical verses—and he used this combination to heighten inner tension,

energy, and brilliance. Demonic drives, restricted
by these steel bands of form, created tension that
seemed ready to burst. Tough restraint and violent
drives were also Brecht's antithesis during his early
period. But to synthesize the two, as Baudelaire
had done, was not Brecht's natural gift.

His unceasing search for synthesis of his dualis-
tic nature may have driven him to Hegel's dialectic
and eventually to Marxism. He never did accom-
plish synthesis, despite a lifetime of searching and
experimenting. His works contain interminably
long and empty passages. His doctrinaire searching, always exaggerated, never moderate or organ-
ically functional, led him to failures that were
sometimes almost childish. One failure was his un-
acknowledged ambition to transform the dramatic
stage into a classroom lectern from which the pro-
fessor instructs, with a few jovialities thrown in here
and there, while the audience has to listen, learn,
and be silent. The paradox of his life is revealed by
the fact that, if one can believe his theoretical writings, he seemed to fear nothing more than to have his
audience swept off its feet, enthusiastic, moved, or
even involved. For twenty years he put down his
theories about the epic theater and *Verfremdung*, as
though he were terrified of emotional reactions. But
in his plays he often abandoned his doctrines by
using little, sentimental, coquettish renderings,
rhetorical declamations, and even genuine dramatic
crescendos and deeply moving plots. Because he
was a dramatist he worked against his theories. His

great success in later years, *Mutter Courage und ihre Kinder (Mother Courage and Her Children),* was a magnificent, classically built, thoroughly healthy play, just as his first success, *The Threepenny Opera,* was a complete denial of all his dramaturgical theories, regardless of what he wrote in his *Experiments* and other theoretical pieces.

One might speculate that his theories about the unemotional and purely instructive theater, designed only to stimulate interest and teach, without passion or fervor, were just sour grapes after his plunge from a stupendous initial success to seemingly permanent failure. There is some truth in this speculation; many truths apply to this obstinate genius and odd schemer who had written the greatest hymns of primordial drives found in modern German literature and who, nevertheless, was a schoolteacher at heart, a clever bargainer who thought he knew how to dicker for his pound but in the end almost lost it. Of Baudelaire's work, too, little of poetic value has survived. But this little has been handed down in the purest form. It is the product of a severe, unerring self-criticism that accepted very little, and all of it perfect in its own way. But much of the monumental fourteen volumes of Brecht's dramatic output will be studied thoroughly ten years from now only by literary researchers and specialists. Among these the non-Marxists will probably far outnumber the Marxists, unless things do change radically in the Philistine literary enterprises east of Potsdam Square. The bulk of his "didactic" works, which at times he so accommodatingly attuned to the whims of those Philistine authorities, will in the long run be intolerable to them. He and his "state" could not understand each other because he, the born immoralist, only acted the part of the Philistine schoolteacher (out of compulsion, cunning, fun, and a little for the sake of irony and self-mockery) where they, the born and unchangeable Philistines, made a show of being "revolutionaries." These attitudes do not go well together. Despite his sadistic and masochistic craving for disciplining and being disciplined, Brecht was an experimenting, restless gadfly. All the potentials of his abundant life, his thirst for learning, searching, and creating, were dammed up in those few decisive years between 1926 and 1933. If we consider Faust and Mephistopheles antitheses of human nature, then Brecht had something of Faust but far more of Mephistopheles: the sinister quality of Brecht's appearance and also the barrenness that overwhelmed him for periods that could stretch into years—for Mephistopheles' spirit is profoundly barren.

The aging Gerhart Hauptmann, for example, once remarked that Brecht's plays struck him as dusty and brittle skeletons. Hugo von Hofmannsthal was one of the few of the older generation who immediately recognized Brecht's genius. If an unbiased edition of Brecht's correspondence could be published, it would probably reveal that the great Viennese poet tried very early to have this young dramatist's works, so different from his own, produced on the stage. I talked several times with Hofmannsthal about Brecht. Hofmannsthal rated Brecht highly, even admired him to some extent, but he spoke of him with the same misgivings I also felt—as if Brecht were a bit spooky. Hofmannsthal finally sponsored a Vienna studio performance of Brecht's first play, *Baal,* at Max Reinhardt's *Theater in der Josefstadt* on March 21, 1926; he also wrote a charming prologue in which he had the actors Hans Thimig, Gustav Waldau, Oskar Homolka, and Egon Friedell (the cultural philospher who occasionally played on Reinhardt's stage) debate about the "modern" theater. Homolka, as spokesman of the "modernists," says: "A play like this constitutes ultimate unity. Here we do not hear cleverly constructed words superimposed on a cleverly constructed scenario. Here gestures and words are a unit. Power explodes from within and fills the new living space it has created." This is a gentle parody of the exalted language of the expressionists of the 1920's but at the same time is, in a nutshell, Hofmannsthal's own formulation.

The Threepenny Opera is not one of Brecht's chief works, either artistically or intellectually; but it is his most brilliant escapade, an ingenious lark, presented with the stupendous power of his songs and Kurt Weill's music. Far more important, among Brecht's earliest dramas, is *Baal,* and during his mature period undoubtedly *Mother Courage.*

Brecht's position after the sensational success of *The Threepenny Opera* and the slump that followed is one of those turns of fate that illuminate a man's life. It revealed the restless experimenter Brecht—his thirst for new orientation, his artificial primitivism and also his genuine simplicity. It also revealed Brecht as a man of letters, an avid reader who gathered his inspiration from every crack and cranny of world literature. He wrote about this in his "Song of the Playwright":

> To be able to show what I see,
> I've read descriptions of other peoples and periods.
> Some pieces I emulated exactly,
> examining their techniques and remembering what I
>   could use.
> I studied the Englishmen's representations of the great
>   feudal lords,
> rich characters,
> who used the world for their development.
> I studied the moralizing Spaniards,
> the Indians, masters of fine emotions,
> and the Chinese who represent family life,
> and the colorful fates of cities.

Brecht kept excellent records. The Englishmen Marlowe and Shakespeare, who portrayed the great feudal lords, inspired him, and on occasion he merely reworked them. The "moralizing Spaniard" Calderón and his spiritual plays evidently contributed significantly to Brecht's conception of his didactic plays; and Gracian y Morales' *Oráculo* is perhaps the source of Brecht's utter amorality, which ended in cynicism. Brecht's theory of the epic theater can be traced to the Indian classical drama, specifically *Sakuntala* by Kalidasa, to mention the most popular. But if one thing influenced him most decisively, it was the theater of East Asia. One can feel it in *Der Jasager (He Who Says Yes)* and *Der Neinsager (He Who Says No)* and, down to the last period, in *Der gute Mensch von Sezuan (The Good Woman of Setzuan)* and *Der kaukasische Kreidekreis (The Caucasian Chalk Circle)*. Probably no other German dramatist has been equally influenced, or for so long a time, by the style of the Asian drama.

To these sources, from which Brecht borrowed directly and frequently, should be added the Irishman J. M. Synge, the Englishmen Gay and Kipling, the Russian Gorki, the German Grimmelshausen, the Czech Hašek, the Frenchman Villon, the Finn Hella Wuolijoki, and others.

The multifaceted Bert Brecht was, among other things, a busy appropriator of literature, a *Literat*. And yet at the end he seemed much the same as he was in 1928. The poet Max Frisch saw him in Zurich in 1948, before Brecht's return to East Berlin. In his *Tagebücher (Diaries)* Frisch wrote of Brecht's "stern, quiet peasant look, often veiled by shrewdness." But then Frisch makes a very beautiful statement which only a person who truly loved Brecht could make: "His almost peasantlike patience, his courage to stand helplessly in an empty field, refusing support; his strength to be modest—possibly without result; but then again his intelligence to grasp the first signs of a useful insight and to let them develop through contradiction; and finally the maturity to take results seriously and live by them regardless of what others think—all these are wonderful lessons which in one hour of instruction easily outweigh a semester. The results, to be sure, belong to him. To see how he has gained them is our gain."

This is the viewpoint of a poet, showing an important, bright aspect of Brecht's nature.

As stated earlier, perhaps not much of his work will survive, but this little, with its infinite tenderness, its powerful, broad, hymnic-sensuous current, its perceptive, quiet elegaic quality, will never be forgotten.

No qualified chronicler of the intellectual and cultural history of this era will fail to include Brecht as an unmistakable, unrepeatable phenomenon of the times, with all his non sequiturs, his trickery, his ambition, his genius, and even his deceptions. No such history would be complete without Bert Brecht.

2

~~~~~~

Small and Great Beginnings

The sixteen-year-old Brecht from Augsburg began publishing like most young German authors: as a feuilletonist, as a book and theater critic for a daily paper. In August 1914, "Notizen über unsere Zeit" ("Notes on Our Times") appeared in the *Augsburger Neueste Nachrichten*. This was followed by a review of a drama by Carl Hauptmann and a story about Rabindranath Tagore, who had just received the Nobel Prize and who had become the favorite poet of the German bourgeoisie. Before 1916 he had several poems and stories published: "Moderne Legende" ("Modern Legend"), "Deutsches Frühlingsgebet" ("German Spring Prayer")— which is worth reading—"Der Fähnrich" ("The Ensign"), "Der belgische Acker" ("The Belgian Field"), "Der Tsingtausoldat" ("The Soldier from Tsingtau"), "Das Lied von der Eisenbahntruppe von Fort Donald" ("The Song of the Railroad Troop from Fort Donald"), and, as early as March 1916, an essay on Frank Wedekind, who apparently meant a great deal to Brecht even then. On October 21, 1919, he started to write theater and movie reviews for the socialist newspaper *Der Volkswille* in Augsburg, and this was the real beginning of his productive work in the field of the theater.

The twenty-one-year-old Brecht was not a theater critic of significance. Undoubtedly, other critics in Augsburg must have written equally adequate, if less rude, reviews. That Brecht at the time was working on one of his greatest dramas, *Baal* (rumor has it that he completed it in four days on a bet with his friend George Pflanzelt), is one of those improbabilities that life produces.

Der Volkswille was the paper of the Independent Socialists. Later, in 1920, it became Communist. Without qualms it printed the sometimes obscene Bavarian crudities of its youthful theater and movie critic. "If the movie houses will be allowed to go on showing such garbage soon no one will go to see films," he wrote in his first feuilletón.

He discusses the then mass-produced "enlightenment films," which were undeniably bawdy. Movie censorship did not then exist. *Der Weg in die Gosse, Das Tagebuch eines Lebemannes,* or *Sinnenrausch (The Road to the Gutter, Diary of a Playboy,* or *Intoxicated with Sex)* were typical titles of these films. Young Brecht comments on them neatly and wittily: "They are earning plenty of money, and everybody learns from them that the lot of the fallen is deplorable but glamorous. As the movies have it, the path of sin leads from a small, badly furnished sewing room through glittering nightclubs (where the poor, danced-out fallen damsels sit on the knees of boozing, affluent, and depraved gentlemen) directly to the ritzy brothels, with their supercolossal scenery right out of the movie *Die Brillianten der Herzogin (The Jewels of the Duchess).* There is no stopping on this path. Police and fellow-man work hand in hand to push these poor victims of male lechery right down into the merry hall of mirrors. The young girls sitting in the movie houses, usually right next to the young men who paid for their tickets, are informed of the fact that once fallen, resistance only leads further downhill, and that all struggle to climb back up, no matter how desperate, is useless and leads only to deeper misery. All bosses are lechers who keep refilling the wineglasses of their secretaries; resistance is useless. If the fallen wretch has a child and the poor worm is starving, the hapless mother, instead of giving it up to an orphanage, sacrifices herself—to the accompaniment of a melodeon—by entering a brothel, while the melodeon, mercifully, can hardly be heard above the sobs of the audience. The young girls are tickled by the exotic pleasures this earth has in store and, thrilled to the core, they imagine the hall of mirrors from *The Jewels of the Duchess* behind the walls of every bawdyhouse. The young men, on the other hand, note with satisfaction 'how easy it is,' that even prominent men do it, and how slight is the risk when one does it as cleverly as the hero on the screen. Thus, each gets his money's worth, business flourishes, 'prostitution' is extended 'by popular demand,' and liberty is the best of all conditions." And, indeed, that's the way these films were. But it is piquant and perhaps more than coincidence that the first known of young Brecht's theater and film reviews was a pitch for censorship.

His review of *Don Carlos* is even more characteristic. It demonstrates the typical rhetorical sentimentality that at that time went under the name of socialism and whose spiritual father was Ludwig

Rubiner. In truth, however, this kind of socialism represents extreme reaction because its exponents did not know how to place a great drama such as Schiller's *Don Carlos* dialectically in its historical perspective. Brecht's review hammers away:

"God knows, I have always loved *Don Carlos.* But I have just read, in Sinclair's *Jungle,* the story of a worker starving to death in the Chicago stockyards. It's about simple hunger, cold, and sickness, which destroy a man as surely as though they were ordained by God. At one point this man has a brief vision of freedom, but he is beaten down with rubber truncheons. I know well enough that his freedom has not the slightest connection with the freedom of Don Carlos, but I no longer can take Carlos' bondage very seriously."

That is the typical "radical" literary "tone" of 1920. Brecht summarizes the theatrical season of 1919–20, the first in which he participated, as follows: "I used to think it amounted to something but I tell you it's nothing less than a scandal. What you see here is your complete bankruptcy, a demonstration of your stupidity, your laziness of thought, and your depravity. No, sir, that's no way to talk, I know: no one can fool you, you've known it all along, and nothing can be done about it."

And here, a few months later, is his judgment about the stage manager:

"The man who leased the Augsburg Stadttheater to milk it for all he can get, today, after many years, knows as much about literature as an engine

driver knows about geography. Last year Herr
Merz taught him something; this year he seems to
be patching the repertory together by himself abid-
ing by the rule that it should cost nothing but draw
a crowd. He threw one terrified look at the empty
house and barked out the orders: Get rid of those
heavy old plays, every one of them! Get some to fill
up the place!"

This statement, certainly not lacking in candor,
probably refers to a play that was performed two
days later, *Alt-Heidelberg (Old Heidelberg)*. The
first sentences of Brecht's reviews are worth reading. He begins: "This garbage contains an utterly
ghastly scene. An old man comes to a moron of a
prince to beg a position, and the moron orders sup-
per for him. The man has been a servant in the offi-
cer corps, and young Germans have so indoctri-
nated him that he can no longer walk with his head
up, talk normally, or think sensibly. And German
mothers and future mothers are moved to tears and
applaud that old, repulsive, undignified, decrepit
wretch, laugh over his loyalty, and enjoy themselves when he crawls on his belly to kiss the hands
of the moron."

The review, it seems, prompted the much-
abused Augsburg Theater to rebel. The actors must
have protested and written a memorandum against
Brecht's criticism. But the critic Brecht made few
concessions. He answered: "As for the terminology,
a concession can be made. Instead of calling it garbage one might say it's swill."

But in principle he stuck to his opinion: "I reject the memorandum as arrogant and impertinent. I fail to see anything in it beyond the documentation of a stubborn insistence to defend, with pointless excuses, the poor accomplishments of the theater. My critical remarks are the most moderate that could be made about those accomplishments and, by themselves, in no way indicate the artistic level of the theater. The latter can be gauged only from my statement that my words indeed are the utmost in moderation and indulgence, the limit of tolerance, that I, as an artist, can reconcile with my conscience."

This statement, which sounds like the swan song of Brecht as a critic, is dated November 27, 1920. In January, 1921, he resigned as critic for the Augsburg *Volkswille*. In reviews of printed, not staged plays, he discussed several more characteristic dramatic works of his expressionistic, pacifist contemporaries: *Die Gewaltlosen (Those without Power)* by Ludwig Rubiner, *Wandlung (Transformation)* by Ernst Toller, and *Hölle, Weg, Erde (Hell, Path, Earth)* by Georg Kaiser. He consistently misspells the names of famous authors. Thus he wrote, for instance, "Hoffmannstal" and "Gerhardt Hauptmann."

But, as mentioned, in the meantime a miracle had occurred: Within a few days he had written the first draft of the drama *Baal*.

His model was Georg Büchner who also, forty years earlier, had been the idol for Gerhart Hauptmann. It is possible, although it has not been proved, that by that time Brecht also was thoroughly familiar with Rimbaud and Verlaine. Much of the end of *Baal* is reminiscent of the catastrophe of the Rimbaud-Verlaine relationship. *Baal* contains much of the spirit of the brutal, powerful Rimbaud, and more perhaps of the vagabond-poet François Villon whose brutality and contriteness haunted the young poet in *The Threepenny Opera* and beyond. Ernst Schumacher, who in 1955 wrote the monumental, standard, toe-the-line Marxist Brecht biography, points to a youthful work by Hanns Johst, *Der Einsame (The Lonesome One)*. Hanns Johst, later the classical writer for the Nazis, had already tainted with anti-Semitism this expressionistic drama of 1920, which was a dramatized chronicle of Grabbe's life. Johst's influence, too, as well as the influence of the megalomaniac Grabbe are undeniable.

Baal is indeed a wild, belching, stinking, pornographic work from the school of the *Sturm und Drang* of Georg Büchner and Grabbe. But still it is the work of a genius—particularly the ballads and the songs. The "Choral vom Großen Baal" ("Chorale of the Great Baal") rises in majestic rhythm. It is unique in German poetry:

> When in his mother's womb sprouted Baal,
> the sky already was so wide and calm and pale,
> young and naked, and immensely marvelous
> as Baal later loved it when Baal came to us.

> And in lust and pain the sky stayed there
> even when Baal slept in bliss, unaware.
> Nights—Baal was drunk, the sky a purple veil;
> mornings—Baal was pious, the sky apricot pale.

And the end of the chorale:

> Baal blinks at the fleshy vultures of the sky
> who wait for his death with hungry zeal.
> Sometimes Baal feigns death. If one swoops nigh,
> Baal, in silence, feeds on vulture for his meal.
>
> Under the dim starlight in this vale of tears,
> Baal with smacking lips the grassland reaps;
> when they're plundered, Baal, while singing, steers
> to the timeless forests where he sleeps.
>
> When the dark womb pulls Baal down to die,
> what's the world to Baal now? Baal is fed.
> He, beneath his eyelid, still has so much sky
> that he has enough when he is dead.
>
> When in the earth's dark womb rotted Baal,
> the sky was still so wide and calm and pale,
> young and naked, and immensely marvelous
> as Baal loved it when Baal lived with us.

Such animistic-animalistic sounds had never been heard before in German literature, or, for that matter, in world literature.

The actual dramatic content of *Baal* hardly goes beyond the expressionist taste of that period: *Baal* is the story of a poet-tramp, seducer, defiler of young girls, pimp, murderer—the plot could have been invented by Klabund. But, far beyond that, it also contains Brecht's animalistic pantheism, a

Panic orgy, a Pantagruelesque spectacle of food-gorging, of insatiable sexuality, and decay—the digestive system of the swampy jungle in which constructive and destructive forces, those of birth and death, cruelly dig into each other in clenched embrace. *Baal* is a unique, chaotic biological hymn, not for sensitive noses and nerves. It is not the best play, but perhaps it is the highest pinnacle ever reached by Brecht. Yet, it was only his first work.

One must not see this great triumph (and this is what *Baal* represents) as a simple product quickly dashed off. To Brecht it never lost its fascination; again and again he reworked it, invented new versions. From the papers he left behind, three versions were published in the Suhrkamp edition; none was effective on the stage.

Lion Feuchtwanger once related how he polished *Baal* with young Brecht. But a man as sharp as Feuchtwanger knew that there was really nothing to slick up. Presumably he placed the drama with his own publisher, Georg Müller—an enormous publishing company printing almost everything of importance from the world of literature of the past two-and-a-half millenia: from Aeschylus to Wedekind, from Lucan to Courteline—often in luxury editions bound in vellum and printed on hand-made paper.

One would think that Brecht's brilliant first drama could have found a nook in this luxurious monster warehouse in which even the owner did not always know his way around. Not so. The play was set in type and proofs pulled. Then something surprising happened that should never happen in a well-run publishing house: the publisher himself read the drama in proof. There was evidently a terrific blowup with the chief editor and managing director. The publisher, of course, did not realize that he had published other books far more suggestive —those by Lucan or Wedekind, for instance. Brecht's rather crude language of questionable taste did not sit well with the publisher. Feuchtwanger reported that the type was killed "after twenty or thirty additional proofs had been pulled for Brecht."

Brecht, who tended to avoid precise information about his life and work (for reasons of his own), never released these proofs, which represented the first real printings, and thereby drove his enormously diligent bibliographer Walter Nubel to desperation. The first edition obtainable to collectors today was published by Gustav Kiepenheuer in Potsdam two years later in 1922. Kiepenheuer remained Brecht's publisher for some time until the gigantic super-capitalistic concern of Ullstein grabbed the wild young Communist to publish his works in its elegant subdivision, Propyläen-Verlag, along with Hasenclever and other revolutionary contemporaries.

Nubel mentions one more early lost item, the *Augsburger Sonette (Augsburg Sonnets),* a private printing which never had a press run. A galley proof is said to have been preserved in Augsburg.

Brecht, punning, called these verses his Achilles
heel (German: Achilles *Ferse*). Significantly, a part
of it was designated as "didactic"—even then! To
quote Hebbel: "We become what we are."

Brecht was under pressure to do something
about his bourgeois career. His father was a well-to-
do industrialist in Augsburg, who wanted his son to
study. Bertolt chose medicine but later changed to
the natural sciences. Most significant, however,
was his chance to discuss problems of the theater in
the seminars of Arthur Kutscher, a friend of Frank
Wedekind and publisher of the latter's complete
works. Kutscher was very knowledgeable in the
history of the theater everywhere. Brecht undoubtedly learned much from him for his later work.

Did he choose medicine only to keep his father
happy? Friends who ought to know say no. Here,
too, his model was Georg Büchner. Büchner, at a
very young age, had become a competent physician,
scientist, and biologist. His road to materialism
(which his popular younger brother Friedrich, a
philosopher, had also taken) branched from these
studies. *Woyzeck* (in the United States better
known as *Wozzek*) could not have been written as
it was without Büchner's studies in psychopathol-
ogy, biology, and physiology. Walter Benjamin
called *Woyzeck*, with good reason, the most consistently materialistic drama in existence: its re-
markably well-defined psychology is based on more
than the brilliance of genius alone. A complete edition of Büchner's works, including his scientific

studies, existed in 1920. Perhaps it influenced Brecht in choosing his formal training.

In any case, his second drama, *Trommeln in der Nacht (Drums in the Night)*, contained little of the sharp, clearly defined psychopathological language of *Woyzeck*.

Drums in the Night is the most dated of Brecht's early plays. It is simply an expressionistic drama in the style of Ernst Toller, Georg Kaiser, or Carl Sternheim. All the exaltations and eccentricities of language in vogue at that time are found in this play. The well-known critic Alfred Kerr (who often was unfair to Brecht, and not always for strictly professional reasons) rightly dubbed Brecht an imitator of the early Georg Kaiser. To judge this today one would have to compare Brecht's *Drums in the Night* with Kaiser's *Von Morgen bis Mitternacht (From Morning to Midnight)*. The filthy language—let us truthfully call it that—is no longer so readily tolerable because here it is not rooted in the great and vital depths as it was in *Baal*. *Baal* was a drama of insatiable gluttony and sexuality, rising to great poetic heights, especially in the ballads. *Drums in the Night* is a harsh, piercing, exaggerated play, often intentionally made filthy.

In this play Brecht turns his attention for the first time to the problem of revolution. The drama takes place during the fight of the Spartacists for the newspaper district of Berlin in January 1919. A drunkard sings:

My brothers are dead
but I was wary.
In November I was red,
but now it's January.

After his return from prison in Africa, Kragler
finds his fiancée Anna, whom he has not seen for
four years, pregnant by another man. Kragler is
asked to join the Spartacists in the newspaper district, where government troops, the Berlin regi-
ment known as "Die Maikäfer" (The Cockchafers),
are shelling with artillery the buildings of one newspaper concern after another: Mosse and Ullstein
first and after a pause also the "Vorwärts" building
which are held by the Spartacists. The Spartacists
are captured or killed.

But Kragler does not join the Spartacists.

Here is the final scene of the drama which
shows the returned Kragler and his fiancée Anna.

KRAGLER: You almost drowned in the tears you shed for
me, and I merely washed my shirt with them! Is my flesh
to rot in the gutter, to help you get an idea of yours into
heaven? Are you drunk?

ANNA: Andree! It doesn't matter!

KRAGLER: *(Does not look into her face, wanders around,
grips his throat)* I've had it up to here! *(Laughs angrily)*
This is just theatricals. Boards and a paper moon, and in the
back the butchery—that alone is real. *(He again walks
about, his arms hang down to the ground, and so he picks up
the drum from the schnapps counter)* They left their drum.
(He strikes it) "Half a Spartacus", or "The Power of Love."
"The Bloodbath in the Newspaper District", or "Every Man
Is Best in His Own Skin." *(Looks up, blinks)* Either with the

shield or without it. *(Drumming)* The bagpipe sounds, the poor people are dying in the newspaper district, the buildings collapse onto them, the morning dawns, they lie on the asphalt like drowned cats. I'm a pig, and the pig is going home. *(He draws a deep breath)* I'll put on a fresh shirt, I've still got my skin. I'll take off my coat, I'll grease my boots. *(Laughs maliciously)* The shouting will all be over tomorrow morning, but I'll lie in bed tomorrow morning and propagate so I won't die out. *(Drumming)* Cutthroats! *(Laughing wildly, almost choking)* Bloodthirsty cowards, that's what you are! *(His laughter chokes his throat, he cannot go on. He staggers about, throws the drum at the moon, which was a lantern, and both drum and moon fall into the river, which contains no water)* Drunkenness and making children. Now comes the bed, the big, white, large bed. Let's go!

ANNA: Oh, Andree!

KRAGLER: *(Leading her toward the back)* You got it warm?

ANNA: But you don't have your jacket on. *(She helps him in)*

KRAGLER: It's cold. *(Puts a scarf around her neck)* Come now! *(They both walk next to each other, without touching, Anna a little behind him. In the air, high, from very far, comes a white, wild shouting from the newspaper district)*

KRAGLER: *(Stops, listens, puts his arm around Anna while standing)* It's been four years.

(While the shouting continues, they leave.)

Thanks to his medical training, Bert Brecht did not have to fight at the front in the First World War but served as an ambulance orderly in a hospital behind the lines. Ernst Bornemann, who was evidently a close friend, reports that it was there

that Brecht witnessed some of the worst mutilation
cases found in Europe. These made an indelible impression on him. He became a pacifist, and his pacifism took a specific direction: the image of the mu-
tilated soldier leading the lame, of the dead soldier
leading the living, is found throughout his works
like a leitmotif. It was the cutting, caustic, piercing,
aggressive pacifism of George Grosz. A poem such
as the "Legende vom toten Soldaten" ("Legend of
the Dead Soldier") in 1920 had the effect of a
bloody satirical George Grosz drawing turned into
words. Undoubtedly those horrid mutilations he
had to witness as an ambulance orderly contributed to his becoming a radical. But radicalism per-
vaded the entire mood of the era, its literature, and
its generation.

In the fifth year of the First World War
(which ended after four years), Brecht has Kaiser
Wilhelm II exhume and remuster the dead soldiers.
One dead soldier is being registered as fit for serv-
ice, and then things begin to happen:

> They pour some fiery booze in the corpse,
> which was decayed in the trench,
> and hung two nurses on his arms
> and a semi-denuded wench.

> And since the soldier stinks of decay,
> a cleric limps ahead,
> he swings the censer on the way—
> no longer stinks the dead.

> Ahead the music plays a march,
> with drums and fifes and brass,

the soldier throws, as he was drilled,
his legs high from his ass.

Two medics put their arms around
and hold him brotherly,
so he won't stumble in the muck,
for that must never be.

In 1919, Brecht became a soldier's deputy in Augsburg during the Bavarian soviet republic, but emerged unscathed when it collapsed.

Five years later, in *A Man's a Man*, he takes the same radical, antimilitaristic line, this time, however, his satire is directed at the so-called British imperialism. After all, as a party-line Communist he can continue his radical antimilitarism only with considerable restrictions and qualifications.

Those who knew him during the period after the First World War describe him singing his own ballads, like his idol Wedekind, in inns and studios, accompanying himself on a guitar or lute, surrounded by friends. Like Wedekind, he composed his own melodies. It is said that, as late as 1928, Brecht sang the songs and ballads of *The Threepenny Opera* for the composer Kurt Weill, indicating his ideas about the tunes before Weill began to work on them.

Very early Brecht formed a productive friendship with Lion Feuchtwanger who describes Brecht at this early period: "When the twenty-year-old Brecht came to me, I was working on a 'dramatic novel.' The term, 'dramatic novel,' started Brecht thinking. He decided that one ought to go much

further in the union of drama and epic that I had
done, and he made repeated efforts to create the
'epic drama.' It was not false modesty that prompted him to call his dramas 'experiments.' These plays
were indeed experiments to make his inner world
visible to the audience in ever different and new
ways. The poet, he felt, had to experiment as Archi-
medes, Bacon, or Galileo had done. All earlier
dramas, even those of Aeschylus and Shakespeare,
were 'experiments' to him. He praised Shakespeare
for his borrowing, without qualms, the ideas and
even the formulations that attracted him, for working them over, recasting them, making them his
own, and changing them in such a way that they
belonged to him completely. The masks of the Chinese theater, the flower path of the Indian drama,
the chorus of the Greek tragedy—everything served
to help his shape his own vision.

"Experiments challenged him, even when they
promised little or no success. Once I drew his attention to the didactic poem of Lucretius, *De rerum
natura*. The hexameters in which the Roman poet
presented the Epicurean teachings gave Brecht the
idea of rewriting the *Communist Manifesto* in hexameters. I pointed out the difficulties, even hope-
lessness, of such an undertaking. But he was ob-
sessed with the idea, would not let go, and we had
to try the experiment. We worked on it for six
weeks before he gave up."

In fact, he never gave up this classicistic attempt and took it up time and again. And he always

referred to Marx, Engels, and Lenin as "our classics."

Brecht continued experimenting with the *Communist Manifesto* in hexameters for at least a quarter of a century. Fragments have been preserved, and Peter Huchel published them in *Sinn und Form,* the journal of the Academy of Arts in East Germany. Here are the famous first lines of the *Communist Manifesto* in hexameters:

Wars are destroying the world and a specter is stalking the rubble,

not emerged from the wars, it has long been observed during peacetime,

threat to the powerful men but a friend to the poor in the cities,

visiting indigent kitchens, deploring their half-empty dishes,

waiting then for the fatigue at the gates of the mines and the shipyards,

calling on people in prison and walking in, lacking a permit,

seen at the desk of the clerks, even heard in the halls of the college,

driving at times giant tanks and flying the death-bringing bombers,

speaking in various languages, silent in many.

Popular guest in the slums and the ghetto, and fear to the palace,

now it has come here to stay, and its name is communism.

One can see that the content of Karl Marx's writings has been substantially modernized. And yet, it was typical of Brecht's traditionalism, humanism, and classicism to tie, at least formally, the latest classical work of materialism, Marx's *Mani-*

festo, to the earliest samples of materialist writings, those of Lucretius. Similarly, Brecht later tied his Communist didactic and educational writings to the ancient Japanese Nō players and to Calderón; and the monumental and most important of his didactic plays, *Die heilige Johanna der Schlachthöfe (Saint Joan of the Stockyards)* (even if half in parody) to the grandiose pathos of Shakespeare's historical dramas.

Brecht's friendship with Feuchtwanger remained productive until Brecht's death. Two of Brecht's dramatic works are specifically acknowledged as the results of that collaboration: the early treatment of Marlowe's *King Edward II,* model for Shakespeare's *Richard III*; and much later, when he was already in exile, his second somnambulistic Joan of Arc drama (the first was his *Saint Joan of the Stockyards*), *Die Gesichte der Simone Machard (The Visions of Simone Machard),* a play about Hitler's invasion of France. Conversely, in Feuchtwanger's *Drei angelsächsische Stücke (Three Anglo-Saxon Plays)* (1927), one of the three dramas, entitled *Kalkutta 4. Mai, vier Akte Kolonialgeschichte* (translated into English as *Warren Hastings*), bears the notation: "This play was written together with Bert Brecht." It is known that in Kaspar Pröckl, a character in Feuchtwanger's novel *Erfolg (Success),* set in Munich, the author portrayed his friend Bert Brecht.

The most important result of their collaboration was undoubtedly the adaptation of Marlowe's

Edward II. It is easy to guess where the two got their inspiration. Presumably not from a thorough study of the Elizabethan theater, because Brecht evidently did not master English until the late years of his exile. Rather, around 1910 the Insel-Verlag published an adaptation of *Edward II* by Alfred Walter Heymel, which attracted attention mostly because of a foreword written by Hugo von Hofmannsthal. Heymel had smoothed out the events of the play, which were difficult to stage in 1910. Brecht and Feuchtwanger did the opposite. They presented the play as brutally as possible, creating a much more powerful, rugged, and original work. A mutual friend describes their collaboration as follows: "Brecht would bring along what he had written, and together they would whittle away at it. Lion was hard as iron. Brecht, being much younger, was prone to ingenious sloppiness, and thus Feuchtwanger complained to me that Brecht could no longer see what he was doing; he had been in Augsburg for two days and had brought back disgustingly smooth verses. It had been a painful job to roughen them up again so they would scan badly—with Brecht, lines have to scan badly." In other words, they worked somewhat like Picasso who often starts out by covering the canvas quite traditionally with a slick and sugary painting, then roughens it up into a provocative, original, eccentric, surrealistic creation.

Familiarity with Marlowe's *Edward II*, however, had still another impact on Brecht and his work. The theme of the drama is the king's incurable homosexual enslavement to the courtier Gaveston, a worthless man who eventually costs the king his crown and his life.

The problem of homosexual enslavement seemed to have intrigued Brecht for years. Early in the 1920's he published in the Munich paper *Der Neue Merkur* the story of a pirate who attaches himself to an ugly, unimportant, aging man and cannot free himself from him. He risks his life, his honor, his crew, and his ships to hold this man. The handling of the plot is reminiscent of Marlowe's *Edward II*.

Later, in *Im Dickicht der Städte (Jungle of Cities)* Brecht experiments once more with a grandiose version of this same theme. The setting is an unrestrained vision of the chaotic jungle city of Chicago—the jungle of depravity, filth, corruption, hunger, sensual appetites, perversions, and great loneliness. This is the backdrop.

It may be pertinent here to point out that in Brecht's monumental dramatic paintings the backdrops tend to be of childlike simplicity and sterility. They are preconceived backdrops, shaped by a literary armchair strategy, lacking genuine local color and even the ambition to provide it; often they are merely "suggested." From such backdrops Brecht, at an early stage, developed that most curious, ambiguous technique which he later called "alienation" and which he tried in many ways, but never quite honestly, to explain.

Brecht is not a man of great original, impressive visions. Where he lacks in genius, he makes it up in cunning. And where cunning does not suffice, a rather primitive man is revealed. His dramatic concepts are always primitive when derived from a visual impression, a milieu, an atmosphere. His vision of Chicago, the "gangster city," in his grotesque *Jungle of Cities*, is derived from cheap crime thrillers, and later, in his *Saint Joan of the Stockyards,* from Upton Sinclair's semiliterary exposés and sensational novels. His lampoons of the British colonial army in *A Man's a Man* come from Kipling's *Barrack-room Ballads*.

All this shows inadequacy on his part, as well as intention—or rather intention born of inadequacy. The backdrop is ironic-dialectic that is supposed to resolve itself into reality. In the midst of a tragic scene, the moon is revealed as a lantern. Slogans and inscriptions in the foyer and on the stage are there to prevent the audience from becoming emotionally involved. At first, it is merely the cheap irony and self-irony found in cabaret skits. But then the matter becomes serious. Doctrines develop from deficiencies. The "epic theater," the "didactic play," and the "alienation" are there to make the audience react in the proper way: they are not to participate emotionally in the play but to think about it. Thus, his "didactic plays" came into being. Communist propaganda came later, as an accessory.

Brecht frequently tried for abstraction. From the complexity of his plots, which in themselves

promise little or no suspense, emerges a structure of
ideas, although by no means a socialist one. The
play *Jungle of Cities* shows two men, a rich Chinese
and a poor employee of a lending library, engaged
in a fight. It is implied that their hate derives from
a homosexual relationship. It would probably be
more accurate to say that they both do their utmost
to confront each other in a fight. The rich Chinese
even signs over his whole fortune to the poor employee because he wants to give him an equal
chance. Others are attracted or repulsed by this
game. The sister of the library employee becomes
the love slave of the Chinese, but he rejects her. In
the end, the poor employee arouses the racial mania
of the American masses against the yellow-skinned
man and they clamor for his lynching. Yet, there is
no direct confrontation: the loneliness in the jungle
of a large city is too great. Not even a fight brings
people into close touch with each other. Here are
two quotations which go to the core. In each, the
Chinese, Shlink, whose life is already lost, speaks to
his opponent, Garga:

Man's isolation is so tremendous that hatred becomes an
unattainable goal. And even with animals it's impossible to
make yourself understood.

And:

Even if you packed a ship so full with human bodies that
it nearly burst, there would still be so much loneliness on
that ship that they'd all freeze to death. Are you listening,
Garga? Yes, loneliness is so overwhelming that there cannot
even be a fight.

A fascinating dramatic motif, perhaps the best Brecht ever found, showing the keenest insight. But one can hardly say that Brecht as much as scratched the surface. The plot is colorful, stark, and intricate enough, but the drama remains merely one of the hundreds of expressionistic plays of the era, possibly even starker than others. It is like a strong musical theme without development.

The tragedy of isolation in the world of today is announced—a powerful theme. But only the first and last scenes come to grips with it. Even the grandiose paradox of the rich man giving the poor his wealth and power to even the chances for the "fight," thus putting himself at the other's mercy, becomes a farce. The word "Chicago" triggers in Brecht the association of a gangster-and-moll atmosphere with disreputable and dirty flophouses and even more disreputable and dirty "saloons," derived from movies or cheap novels. His brain and his pen follow this path, and he forgets the rest—the more important insights.

This play, although it was successful in an era when expressionist plays automatically succeeded, actually is a failure. Georg Kaiser, in his best years, could have done something far more significant with it.

From 1922 on, Brecht worked as stage director with Reinhardt. During a short period Max Reinhardt looked at the expressionist drama as something that possibly might work for him and his theater. One episode, reported by eyewitnesses, illustrates Reinhardt's conscientiousness: hour after hour he sat through Brecht's rehearsals, asking only an occasional question, modestly, not as one who is in charge but as one who is interested in learning. Disappointingly, it was also his conscientiousness that made Reinhardt stop experimenting with the new drama because he felt that it would always remain foreign to him, that it would not fit into the atmosphere of his theaters, and that he would not fit into the atmosphere of expressionism. There was much modesty and self-discipline in this decision. Business considerations may also have played a part.

In 1923 Brecht was awarded the Kleist Prize by Herbert Ihering, a distinguished critic for the Berlin *Börsenkurier,* who for the rest of his life remained Brecht's spokesman. Ihering's announced reason for the award is interesting: he placed Brecht's plays between the individualism of the old bourgeois psychological theater of, say, Ibsen, and the generalizations of expressionism—as plays portraying individuals living, interacting, and responding to society.

During the following years, from 1924 to 1926, Brecht worked on the comedy *A Man's a Man,* with which Ihering had evidently been familiar at the time he awarded Brecht the Kleist Prize. The play is a satirical farce about the interchangeability of men, the possibility of modern times to "remodel" individuals, which is to say, to change their fundamental individuality. Brecht exemplifies his thesis

in a poor English packer, Galy Gay, in India or
Burma. British colonial soldiers seize and recruit
him for the British army to replace one of their
comrades who had disappeared in a pagoda after
a theft. The remodeling proceeds rapidly, presented as a farce. Brecht explains it in a comment
spoken by one of the participants in the course of
the play:

> Herr Bertolt Brecht states: A Man's a Man.
> You can say this, of course, and anyone can.
> But Herr Bertolt Brecht further decrees:
> You can do with a man whatever you please.
> Here is a man, rebuilt tonight like an automobile
> without losing thereby a thing in the deal.
> The man is politely being requested,
> with emphasis but without being molested,
> to kindly conform to the general wish
> and to let go of his private fish.
> And whatever he is remodeled into,
> it will satisfy and well enough do.
> We can, if we only approach it right,
> change a man to a butcher just overnight.
> Herr Brecht hopes that the ground under your toe
> will be melting away like snow,
> and from longshoreman Gay you will gather thus
> that life on this planet is hazardous.

A Man's a Man, just as *Jungle of Cities,* contains an interesting ideological base: that contemporary man can be remodeled and made usable in
any way desired. Again, Brecht hardly let this idea
gain form and life. He superimposes on it an eccentric military farce with all sorts of effective, but
more often flat, barracks horseplay. If the comedy

were presented with genuine humor and without the eccentric tomfoolery, which here is especially superfluous, it might be entertaining. But this approach evidently had never been tried, although the play was performed several times "expressionistically"; thus, it leads a shadowy existence like *Jungle of Cities*. On Brecht's orders it was played with masks and on three-foot-high buskins.

It is noteworthy how Brecht, who published volumes of ideological studies and essays on drama, kept missing the essence of a specific problem. The remodeling of an individual into a machinelike soldier is a fact that has always existed and probably will exist as long as there are soldiers; it is not unique to our time. That modern man is specifically susceptible to being remodeled could have been better demonstrated by any example other than the military. Brecht's Marxist biographer Schumacher points out the process of abstraction peculiar to capitalism, as predicted by Marx, a process that remodels not only man but also his labor into an abstract commodity. But those who quote Marx ought also to note how Brecht's intellectual insecurity makes him antirevolutionary and profoundly reactionary—here, in *Jungle of Cities,* and even later in many of his propagandistic "didactic" plays. The process of stripping a man of his individuality is here satirized. Later, in his didactic play *Die Maßnahme (The Measures Taken),* Brecht glorified the same process as the essence of the Communist propaganda, and again he did it out of the same intellectual insecurity and the same sadistic predilection for the inhumane and antihuman which he shares with Baudelaire.

Brecht here missed perhaps the most significant dramatic motif of our time, which he should have seen, had he been more of a visionary. Today, men are in fact being remodeled and mechanized, not so much by capitalism, as Marx had erroneously thought—because man's mechanization in industry decreases as the factories themselves become automated—but rather by Communism which seems to have developed methods of completely remodeling, of totally transforming personality, and of brainwashing in a manner never dreamed of by capitalism.

A Man's a Man has been called a satire on British colonial imperialist policies, and this interpretation is supported by the text—for the superficial reader. For the less superficial reader this anti-imperialism turns out to be nothing but a rather mechanical reversal of Kipling's heroic-primitive poetic imperialism. This play owes its style and atmosphere entirely to Kipling's songs and colonial stories. Brecht was inspired by a thrill in brutality, which soon afterwards led him to adapt John Gay's *Beggar's Opera*. In *A Man's a Man* we find the seed of Brecht's "Kanonenlied" ("Song of the Heavy Cannon")—and the jubilant applause that greeted that song at the opening night of *The Threepenny Opera* marked, as it were, Brecht's breakthrough to world fame.

Before discussing Brecht's most inspired book, his *Manual of Piety,* I should like to comment on a few unimportant, practically unknown but characteristic and, in fact, movingly humorous one-act plays.

Two of these, *Die Kleinbürgerhochzeit (The Bourgeois Wedding)* and *Er treibt einen Teufel aus (He Expels a Devil),* were intended for the popular touring groups. These plays are reminiscent of Ludwig Thoma's Bavarian one-act plays which he wrote for his peasant theater and of parts written for the actor Queri who was even more earthy than Thoma. Unfortunately, the popular Munich folk actor Karl Valentin, whom Brecht admired and with whom he remained in personal touch, never included these plays in his repertory. Even more unfortunately, they were performed— certainly not without young Brecht's approval— in much too sophisticated theaters where they flopped. One might try the test even today: one of the popular Munich ensembles ought to stage these one-act plays. Never was Brecht closer to the genuinely popular folk theater, or to a natural appeal to a mass audience. This was also the time when he wrote an essay about the folk drama—an essay still worth reading. But that was the way things went with him: everything he did was thought in pieces rather than thought through and traced back to its elementary origins. His inner insecurity hardly ever allowed him to rely on his own instincts, and this was exactly what this ingenious animalistic man should have relied upon. And so he developed the semiabstract, schematized, "didactic" play, instead of the folk play for the masses, which was easily within his grasp.

Two other one-act plays are less interesting. *Lux in Tenebris* takes place in a street of the red-light district in Augsburg. In a tent, in the middle of that street, the humanitarian Paduk is displaying wax models of the most terrible venereal diseases, to warn people and to make a buck. The stage, then, is set cleverly enough. This farce, too, might be staged with humorous effect—although it probably could not be shown today in the Rhineland, Bavaria, or anywhere else in Germany because "that's not the way things are." The fourth piece is an allegorical dialogue between a beggar and a king, *Der Bettler oder Der tote Hund (The Beggar or the Dead Dog)*.

But now to discuss the little book that appeared in 1927 and that established Brecht's lasting fame as a great poet; a great book of poems and songs—his *Manual of Piety*.

There is an ironic footnote to this work, too: the book was first published at the Propyläen-Verlag of Ullstein—a publisher who also purchased the right to all of his earlier and the most important of his later works. The revolutionary Brecht had comfortably ensconced himself in the center of "exploiting capitalism," in order to live a good life, precisely as the hero of *Drums in the Night* disregarded the Spartacist fighters in the Berlin news-

paper district and enjoyed himself in a warm bed
with his girl. But Brecht, as was his custom, did it
not without spouting some bitter and cynical truths.
Thus, with his truck-driver's leather jacket and his
silk shirts, he became a celebrity in "Berlin-West"
—the culturally sophisticated residential and theater section of the Berlin bourgeoisie.

He knows what he owes his exacting audience,
for he is now a well-known man. He is something of
a German Rimbaud—at a time when Rimbaud was
considered one of the greatest poets in France.
Twice Brecht adapts *Le Bateau Ivre (Drunken
Ship)*, one of Rimbaud's principal works. And he
goes beyond Rimbaud: almost routinely, as others
turn to office work, he turns to rotting carrion, dung,
and the decomposing green corpse of the drowned.
He does his best to shock the Philistine—and the
Philistine is duly shocked and pleasantly thrilled.

But then it becomes increasingly evident that
this modern concocter of terror in 1925 is a true
demon like the Indian god Siva who lives in graves,
clad in the skins of dead rats, cats, and snakes—but
who also notices in his grave how a plant seed
bursts open, dies, and is reborn again, and who is
able to conduct dances and sing hymns to this tune
of decay and rebirth that makes the world listen.

The *Manual of Piety* contains songs and verses
that are as enigmatically sublime as anything that
man has ever sung, such as the "Großer Dankcho-
ral" ("Great Thanksgiving Chorale"), which opens
with these lines:

Praise be to night that envelops you darksome and vast!
Come all, raise your eyes
High to the skies:
your day already has passed.

Praise be to grass and to beasts—lo! beside you they live
       and they die!
Grass and beasts too,
—behold!—live like you,
and, like you, they must also die.

Praise be to the tree that in joy grows from rot to the sky!
To rot—praise be,
and praise to the rot-eating tree,
but also, praise to the sky.

The chorale ends with two lines that are eminently characteristic of Brecht:

> You do not count,
> and you can die without concern.

Some of his most tender love poems are included in this slender volume, for example his "Erinnerung an Marie A." ("Remembrance of Marie A."). It always seems to me a dreamy copy of a Chinese poem or scroll, but this does not diminish its beauty. The book also contains the magnificent ballad of Cortez and his companions engulfed by the jungle. Further included is the unique "Bericht vom Zeck" ("Report from Zeck"), which has no parallel in German literature. Today when admiring someone like Clemens Brentano, or E.T.A. Hoffmann, we ought to remember that a poet in our own time plumbed the ultimate resources of German romanticism; Brecht does this in "Report

from Zeck." Also to be found in the *Manual of Piety*
is the ballad "Vom ertrunkenen Mädchen" ("On
the Drowned Girl"). Brecht deliberately takes one
of Shakespeare's memorable scenes in *Hamlet,* the
Queen's report of Ophelia's drowning, and renders
it in strikingly free paraphrase:

> And when she had drowned, and floated by
> from the brook to the larger stream,
> like opal gleamed a miraculous sky,
> as if the corpse to redeem.
>
> And seaweed and algae weighted on her,
> as she sank, in their clutching grip;
> coolly the fish at her legs were astir
> and followed her final trip.
>
> The sky, in the evening, was dark as smoke,
> and its stars held suspended the light.
> But it was bright when the morning broke
> so that even for her there was day and night.
>
> And when the water had wasted her body bare,
> it befell that God, as time passed, forgot—
> her face first, then her hands, and finally her hair
> became rot in the river's abundant rot.

Poetry such as this endures. These verses must
be kept in mind when the cynical wisdom of the
songs in *The Threepenny Opera,* which make up the
true value of that play, is judged.

3

The Threepenny
Opera
and Its
Consequences

In 1920 Sir Nigel Playfair staged a new production of the almost two-hundred-year-old *Beggar's Opera* by John Gay, with music by the Anglicized Hamburg composer Pepusch, at the Lyric Theater in London's Hammersmith district. He had an enchanting actress for the part of Polly which had always been a choice part for young attractive actresses if they could measure up to that classical soubrette role. Playfair had enlisted the services of an excellent contemporary artist for the costumes and decorations. The production was a huge success in London, as the *Beggar's Opera* has always been when dusted off and newly staged.

The old play, first performed in the concert gardens of Vauxhall, was originally conceived as a sharp parody of Friedrich Handel's heroic operas, which at that time were being shown in the Royal Theatre at the Haymarket. The punch was well placed. The famous composer was greatly damaged both artistically and financially by the success of the *Beggar's Opera*. Hit tunes from the operetta were hummed and whistled everywhere in the streets of London. These old songs were revived even more recently, after Brecht and Weill, by Benjamin Britten.

The old *Beggar's Opera* already contained the parodying "solemn" choruses that were so effectively used in the Brecht-Weill adaptation—particularly the impressive final chorus in the first version of Brecht's *Threepenny Opera*. From the stand-

point of lyrics and music it is perhaps the most
beautiful piece in that work:

> Don't persecute injustice, for it will
> soon freeze to death and perish anyway.
> Think of the darkness, of the awesome chill
> here in this vale of grieving and dismay.

Hogarth had painted a scene from the old *Beggar's Opera* and also a portrait of the first Polly. The
two paintings rank among Hogarth's major works.
Gay himself was probably inspired by the bitter,
savage, burlesque satire of Hogarth's etchings. Hogarth was about thirty when the *Beggar's Opera*
was first staged. Today his brilliant etchings seem
like counterparts of Gay's works.

What prompted Brecht to reach back to the
Beggar's Opera and thus achieve an international
breakthrough for himself and the composer Kurt
Weill?

The year 1928, when *The Threepenny Opera*
appeared, was believed to be the two-hundreth anniversary of the *Beggar's Opera*, and this supposedly was Brecht's motive for refurbishing the old
work. Another version, from the usually well-informed Schumacher, has it that there was a Handel
renaissance around 1920, which Bert Brecht felt to
be reactionary and which he wished to counteract.
The motive for the new *Threepenny Opera*, then,
would have been in essence the same as for the old
Beggar's Opera.

But this is doubtful. Certainly, some passages
in the text and music of *The Threepenny Opera*

may be interpreted as parodying Handel. However, only music experts will recognize them. Handel's music is so remote from any contemporary concern that it can hardly be called a dangerous reactionary factor that requires counteraction. No doubt Brecht, on occasion, may have given this or a similar explanation. But that's another story, and part of his character.

The most obvious explanation is probably the one closest to the truth: Brecht, like the rest of us, had read about the enormous success of the London performance. He became familiar with the plot through newspapers and magazines, and, understandably enough, was fascinated by the material. He asked his loyal associate Elisabeth Hauptmann to translate the original text for him. Then he became enthusiastic and began to work, hoping to repeat the London success in Berlin. That hope was fulfilled because of his talent, his genius, his good instinct for the mood of the time, and above all because of his magnificent musical associate Kurt Weill.

It was the time of the early fad for "musicals" in Berlin. Today the word "musical" is used only in the American sense, meaning an expensive, spectacular show, a more or less unified entity. At that time it was something different. Max Reinhardt produced as "musicals" Somerset Maugham's comedy *Victoria,* Fritz von Unruh's *Phäa,* and an American Broadway hit, *Artists,* with added songs, music, dancing, and various amusements. In this kind

of production Reinhardt was a virtuoso. Georg
Kaiser, next to Brecht the finest dramatist of the
time (and occasionally his superior), wrote a "revue" called *Zwei Krawatten (Two Neckties)*, which
was successfully performed with the charming music by Mischa Spolianski, starring Hans Albers, and
using dancing girls. Kaiser also wrote a jazz opera,
*Der Zar lässt sich photographieren (The Tsar Has
His Picture Taken)*, with music by Kurt Weill. The
biggest hit of the 1928 season was one of the most
delightful "revues" ever presented: *Es liegt in der
Luft (It's in the Air)* by Spolianski, with Marlene
Dietrich and Margot Lion, in the *Theater am Kur-
fürstendamm*.

In fact, the success of *The Threepenny Opera*
was "in the air." Brecht and Weill had many models
—but not only in 1728 London and 1928 Berlin.
Brecht drew from the verses of the fifteenth-cen-
tury vagabond-poet and highwayman François Villon. Again, as in *A Man's a Man,* Brecht wrote soldier songs in the style of Kipling's *Barrack-Room
Ballads*.

All his models—Gay, Hogarth, Villon, and
Kipling—can be sensed in the fabric of *The Three-
penny Opera*'s final version. As noted, Brecht was a
Literat who rarely wrote without literary models.

And yet, his final creation was entirely original
and contemporary, entirely in the style of the cynical 'twenties, entirely Berlin-West 1928, with its in-
solence, its Bohemian elegance, and its polished dialectic. At the same time, the play was a seismo-

graph of the threatening future which—despite all cynicism, luxury, pleasure-seeking elegance, caustic wit, and the arrogance of a metropolis standing near the center of the cultural world—already foreboded the guillotine that was, a few months later after Black Friday at the New York stock exchange, to crash down on people everywhere. The songs of *The Threepenny Opera* get their reckless impact from cynicism at the brink of disaster—an impact still felt today. For it was this world crisis that brought Hitler on the scene, resulting in the Second World War and the collapse of old Germany. A foretaste of all this is evident in the songs of *The Threepenny Opera*, just as the cynical aphorisms of Chamfort anticipate the death of another epoch, the rococo, in the French Revolution. In a notable review, Herbert Ihering contrasted *The Threepenny Opera* with the charming, somewhat decadent gala revue *It's in the Air*, and dubbed the Brecht piece "the play of the time." Future literary criticism may place Brecht's and Weill's *Threepenny Opera* next to Beaumarchais' *Marriage of Figaro*. Both are relatively harmless-sounding, cynical, and witty signals of a cataclysm.

All this does not change the fact that *The Threepenny Opera* is only an episode, and not even a decisive one, in Brecht's life work. Yet, the work contains much that expresses Brecht's innermost self—more than any other of his plays. If there exists a true, deep confession by this poet who profoundly hated, despised, and caricatured confes-

sions, then it can be found in two stanzas from the
songs of *The Threepenny Opera,* sung by Mack the
Knife, murderer, rapist, and thief:

> The bold adventurers with their daring looks
> and with their readiness to risk their hides,
> who freely speak the truth and tell no lies,
> so Philistines can read some daring books:
> Just watch them evenings, shivering in their room,
> when they with frigid wives go wordlessly to bed,
> afraid of gossip that may have been spread—
> they peer into the future full of gloom.
> I ask you: isn't such existence hell?
> Only the affluent live truly well.

> I easily can see myself on top,
> a man alone, and made of special stuff,
> but when I saw such people close enough
> I told myself: Such thoughts you'd better drop.
> Want brings not only wisdom, also chores;
> and daring not just wisdom, also sighs.
> Now you were lonesome, poor, and daring, wise,
> now greatness, go to hell—I want no more.
> The cause of happiness is not so hard to tell:
> Only the affluent live truly well.

The malicious could say that this is no longer
Mack the Knife speaking, but Bert Brecht himself,
all of him—at least the Brecht of 1928. But a man,
especially a man like Brecht, has many facets. The
stanzas show one facet of Bert Brecht, and that
one in its entirety. It speaks in his favor that once
in his writings he truthfully revealed that facet of
his character. But it is by no means all of Brecht.

The Threepenny Opera, of course, is a paean
to cynicism, amorality, and anarchistic violence—

it is indeed a paroxysm of delight over these. It remained for the platitudinous literary nit-pickers—to use a term of Rimbaud's much admired by Brecht and by us—to discover the supposedly soft, wounded heart of social compassion behind this thorny exterior.

And indeed it was discovered by his socialist friends. They couldn't possibly be satisfied with him. *The Threepenny Opera* was not a true socialist drama, no matter how one looked at it. It was a universal blasphemy—against bourgeoisie and socialism alike. The Marxist Schumacher rightly complains that Brecht did not treat his material "dialectically": he did not show the sharks of 1928, the executives of large corporations, but those of the eighteenth century—the highwaymen, pimps, and petty capitalists of panhandling. Brecht finally gave in as he always did in similiar cases. With a Machiavellian sleight of hand, which intrigues us to this day, he tried to give the whole thing a dialectic Marxist twist: it was this sleight of hand that caused the notorious litigation over the film rights of *The Threepenny Opera*.

A movie company, Nerofilm, had bought the rights to a movie version of *The Threepenny Opera*, undoubtedly for a considerable sum. They engaged a perfect director for the project—G. W. Pabst, probably a socialist himself. At any rate, he had been the director of the sufficiently radical socialist movie *Freudlose Gasse (Joyless Street)* with Greta Garbo. Brecht had reserved the rights to furnish the screen scenario adapted from *The Three-penny Opera*.

And furnish he did. It took care of all those objections and criticisms of his friends and party comrades—actually Brecht was not at that time a member of the German Communist party. Not then, and not later, until 1933. Perhaps he never became an actual member of the Party. As an immigrant to the United States he testified under oath that he was not and never had been a member. We can believe that the German Communist party placed no value on counting Brecht as one of its members, which would have detracted from his propaganda useful-ness and his world fame in the Western countries.

Nevertheless, if we are correctly informed, Brecht tried to change the plot of the screen story of *The Threepenny Opera* considerably, trans-planted the story to an imaginary present, and re-made Mack, the scoundrel and whoremonger of the eighteenth century, into a bank president of 1928. Of course, the movie company protested that it could not use this version and produced a scenario that followed closely the plot of the stage version. Brecht brought action. The attorney for the de-fendant at the trial, entirely in the style of the play, asked at the beginnings of the proceedings: "What sum does Herr Brecht demand for withdrawing his action?" This would have made a good scene for *The Threepenny Opera*.

But Brecht seemed outraged. Contrary to the whimsical style of his *Threepenny Opera*, things

suddenly were bitterly serious and Brecht became
the great revolutionary going ahead full blast.

I do not know how the trial ended. Brecht
must either have withdrawn his action or lost his
case. G. W. Pabst did not give in to Brecht—in
court. But being a good leftist and friend, he in-
serted a series of scenes in which he did, in fact,
show Mack as a bank president as Brecht had
wished. The movie was shown in all German movie
houses and was a huge success.

The comedy was followed by a farce. Alfred
Kerr who, growling like an old tomcat, malicious
though not poisonous, had reviewed *The Threepenny Opera* more or less favorably as an "adaptation," suddenly published a sensational accusation:
one song in *The Threepenny Opera,* he alleged,
was a plagiarism from François Villon, as translated by Karl Lothar Ammer using the pseudonym
Klammer.

The eminent Kerr was a master in pulling such
tricks. It had been common knowledge among the
literary colony that one of the songs in *The Threepenny Opera,* from a scene in a brothel, was a word-
for-word loan from a poem by Villon as translated
by K. L. Ammer. This was no more interesting to us
than the fact that Goethe had taken a section in
*Erzählungen deutscher Ausgewanderten (Tales of
German Emigrants)* from the old memoirs of a certain Bassompière.

Brecht replied, not without humor, that, yes,
he had taken a few verses of Villon as translated by

Ammer without acknowledging the source. On the other hand, he had credited in his text the "Song of the Heavy Cannon" as a translation "from Kipling," while in fact it was Brecht's original. Thus, things had come out evenly.

No doubt, it is correct to say that the "Song of the Heavy Cannon" is not a translation "from Kipling." Nevertheless, I do not think that the credit line "from Kipling" was entirely unjustified. It is all a matter of degree. The "Song of the Heavy Cannon" is certainly "from Kipling," just as a good part of *A Man's a Man* is "from Kipling," even though it contains no literal translation.

With this farce, the battle of *The Threepenny Opera* was over. It was a big and well-earned triumph for Brecht and Weill. But now Brecht was destined to live through the most severe disappointment with his Berlin-West public from whom he had had so much acclaim.

4

Epilogue to
The Threepenny
Opera

The Threepenny Opera, in addition to its sequel, The Threepenny Opera Trial, also had an epilogue.

To begin with, the emigrant Brecht—during the years after the fall of Hitler's Germany—added several topical encore stanzas to some of his songs; these stanzas remain relatively unknown.

This is traditional procedure. In the old Viennese popular theaters, during the time of Nestroy and Raimund in the first half of the nineteenth century, the main actor—who was usually the author himself—sang some specially written encore stanzas of a more or less harmless topical nature when the applause was heavy. In the last stanza he usually thanked the audience, to signal the end of the song; then the play would continue or the curtain would come down. The actor Alexander Girardi, last heir of genuine folk tradition of the old Vienna stage, still sang these encore stanzas, which he himself devised. This was after the turn of the century. The practice was then taken up by Karl Kraus in his popular readings from Nestroy. His encore stanzas, which he sang to the original music with piano accompaniment, were usually pointed political satires. This probably prompted Brecht to take up the good old tradition in his own fashion—perhaps after the Second World War when he stayed in Vienna and had become an Austrian citizen. He wrote three topical satirical encore stanzas to the famous "Song of the Heavy Cannon." Two are as follows:

Karl was in the Party, Fritz in the S.A.
and Bert got the job he liked best.
But all of a sudden all this was passé
and they traveled to East and to West.
Schmitt from the Main
wants the Ukraine
and Krause wants Paree.
And if it did not rain,
and if they could refrain
from bothersome collisions
with enemy divisions,
Herr Meier from Berlin would get
Bulgaria, certainly.

Schmitt didn't come back and the Reich was done in,
there were rats and dead bodies galore;
but right in the rubble of ruined Berlin
they talked of the *third* world war!
Cologne is wrecked
and Hamburg sacked,
and Dresden an omelette.
But if the Americans
unleash the hurricanes
perhaps against the Russians,
this may start repercussions,
and Krause in his field gray garb
may rule the world yet.

Today, these lines are dated but they still have
validity.

Brecht also replaced the "Ballade vom ange-
nehmen Leben" (translated as "The Secret of Gra-
cious Living") by a new one written to existing music by Kurt Weill who had died in New York. It was
aimed primarily at Göring and Keitel and is an allu-
sion to the Nuremberg trial of war criminals. Brecht,

in his new position as the classical dramatist of German Marxism, undoubtedly wanted to eliminate that song swiftly and quietly because it contained pointed self-confessions of a nihilistic and cynical nature. But the result was not particularly successful.

The strongest encore stanza he added to the "Ballade, in der Macheath Abbitte leistet" ("Ballad in Which Macheath Begs Pardon of All"). Here are the last verses of that stanza:

> And those who drove you to war and to shame
> and laid you on stones full of blood—
> those who pressed you to murder and robbery,
> are now whining for pity,
> stuff up their mouths with the debris
> left over from a beautiful city.
> And if of forgetting they yap
> and if they forgiveness propose,
> then smash their dirty trap
> with iron hammer blows.

Above all, the Communist Bert Brecht now considered it necessary to write for the whole comedy a final scene that was to stress the work's alleged class-war character, which had been so evasive. In the new final scene, the two "bourgeois" and criminals of the play, the brigand Macheath—his bourgeois character is repeatedly emphasized in the pedantic detailed dramaturgic and stage notes in the appendix of the book edition—and the capitalistic bloodsucker of London's beggars, Peachum, are reconciled:

> In the end, they sit together
> to consume the poor man's bread . . .

The last, incidentally very effective, stanza of the final chorus written to the melody of "Und der Haifisch, der hat Zähne" ("Moritat of Mack the Knife"), had already been rewritten for *The Threepenny Opera* movie:

> And some people live in darkness,
> and some others live in light,
> and you see those in the daylight,
> not the others in the night.

A beautiful final chorus—yet, the original one was more beautiful still.

But it was not Brecht's habit ever to give up plans after they had matured to a certain point. It was mandatory that the material of *The Threepenny Opera* be given a dialectical twist. Sooner or later it had to be reworked into an explicit satire against "bloodsucking" modern capitalism. What he had not been able to achieve in *The Threepenny Opera* movie was now to be presented as a novel: the final Marxist remodeling of this un-Marxist theme. Thus he wrote *The Threepenny Novel*, evidently in Prague or, at any rate, under the influence of his exile experiences in Czechoslovakia: a primitive *roman à clef,* in which Anton Bat'a and the Bat'a concern—one of the world's largest shoe factories, supplying Asia with shoes—is caricatured rather crudely. It is not doing an injustice to Brecht to characterize the novel as an attempt that never came off. Brecht simply was no story teller.

The Threepenny Novel squeezed the last drop

from *The Threepenny Opera*. Only in exile did he
consider the theme exhausted

The time in Berlin was the crucial period in
the life of the poet Bertolt Brecht. It is rarely seen
in its proper perspective, because in the midst of
this fluid phase came the enormous success of *The
Threepenny Opera*—seemingly a focal point in
Brecht's life but actually only an episode and, in
any case, only one of the many avenues which
Brecht then explored: a hymn to the animal in man,
to cynicism, avarice, greed. All this is satirical only
to a limited extent. Schumacher aptly notes that
the satire of social criticism in *The Threepenny
Opera* is far less pointed than that of the two-
hundred-year-old original *Beggar's Opera* of John
Gay and Pepusch.

We leave it to the psychologists to decide
whether the cynicism of *The Threepenny Opera*
was genuine or affected. But it was—along with its
nihilistic and amoral tendencies—unquestionably
one of the paths which Bertolt Brecht took on his
way to Marxism and finally to Communism.

Another path was his love of Machiavelli and
of Jesuitism, the word being used here in the popular manner, which has little to do with the real
Jesuit order (Brecht himself came from an old
Protestant family). A part of this direction was his
deep-seated craving to obey, to subordinate himself spinelessly to a doctrine, an organization, a
"church."

Brecht went the typical way of a convert who

comes from a life in which he has lost his direction and knows no way out, and demands above all one thing from the faith to which he has turned: that the burden of free will, indeed of all moral responsibility, be taken from his shoulders. Only in this light can his early "didactic works" be understood. The poet, cold and increasingly lost in abstractions, made no attempt to portray the human content of socialism until much later, presumably under the influence of Gorki's *The Mother*.

However, all this does not explain Brecht's turning to the strictly doctrinaire Marxist drama. It is true that the dialectical cynicism of the Party showed him the shortest way from *Baal* and *A Man's a Man* to such didactic plays as *The Measures Taken*. It is also true that his search for firmer ground was prompted by some resounding failures of his dramatic imagination, some colossal defeats in Berlin. And it is certainly true that Brecht had not been as angry at the capitalistic public before it had handed him these painful defeats.

I don't know what lay hidden in that invisible gap between tremendous success and patent failure —possibly private conflicts.

The private life of Bertolt Brecht, who after all was a representative figure of that period, has been kept secret to a ridiculous extent. I certainly do not wish to probe into intimate details; nor is it my purpose to have school children of the future memorize dates of Bert Brecht's romances, as earlier they had to memorize the dates of Goethe's love life. But some essential facts would be welcome—they are not available.

It is known that at the time of *The Threepenny Opera* Brecht was close to the beautiful and talented actress Carola Neher. She had been formerly linked with the poet Klabund who died at an early age. Carola Neher was cast to play the leading role of Polly in *The Threepenny Opera.* It was said that she had taken ill, and at the last moment the gifted actress Roma Bahn, wife of the producer Karlheinz Martin, took over that coveted part for the world premiere and played it exquisitely—many thought better than Carola Neher, who later played it on the stage as well as in the movie. The leading part in *Saint Joan of the Stockyards,* staged much later by Gustaf Gründgens in Hamburg, was still clearly written for Carola Neher.

But then the actress Helene Weigel came into the life of the poet. She shared his life through the decades of successes, sufferings, and setbacks until his death.

Helene Weigel, whom I first saw in *The Mother,* was a fine, warm, charming actress, in addition to being an artist of tragic stature. What part she played in Brecht's life one can only guess. His drawing closer to the orthodox Party line falls into this critical period; more than once I have seen women lead their men to Party discipline: woman's eternal desire for "security," even in the vaguest forms, seems overpowering. But this is only a hypothesis. The fact is that after 1945, and after

Brecht's move from Vienna to East Berlin, it was Helene Weigel and not Brecht who officially became the manager of the *Theater am Schiffbauerdamm*—a position which, undoubtedly, had been requested and granted as the main condition for the move.

Bert Brecht and his wife continued in honor the tradition of that old theater in which the world premiere of *The Threepenny Opera* had taken place in 1928. The ensemble of the theater had well-earned successes in Paris and London. Even today, after Brecht's death, it is one of the best German theaters. The admirable care and meticulousness with which Brecht produced plays here—and not only his own—is evidenced by his notes and by recollections of his closest assistants published after his death. In the meantime, Helene Weigel had developed into a theater manager who was sure of herself and well aware of her goals. Her creation of the title role in *Mother Courage* was the highpoint of that theater. Today it proudly bears the name of "The Berlin Ensemble on Bertolt Brecht Square."

What happened to Carola Neher is unknown. She evidently first went to Prague in 1933. As a Party Communist, the road to Moscow was open to her. However, she presumably was trapped by one of Stalin's *agents provocateurs*. She was last seen in a Moscow prison by Margarete Buber-Neumann who described Carola Neher as just as beautiful and enchanting as ever.

At the world premiere of *Saint Joan of the*

Stockyards, in 1959, I met the leading actress, the young and talented Hanne Hiob, a daughter of Brecht by an early marriage with Marianne Zoff whose father had been a well-known Vienna theater critic.

These are some of the fragments known of Brecht's private life.

5

~~~~~~

Theory
and Practice
of the
"Didactic Plays"

*D*as Badener Lehrstück vom Einverständnis (*The Baden-Baden Cantata of Acquiescence*), written for the composer Paul Hindemith and the cause of a big scandal at the 1929 Baden-Baden music festival, is not the first in the series of Brecht's didactic plays. However, it shows the essence of his technique used in the didactic plays, the origins and traditions, what is new and old in these plays, his metaphysics and his antimetaphysics. It reveals, perhaps more than anything else, the true nature of Brecht.

The Baden-Baden play rests on a broad foundation. The legend of the dying and transfigured man who receives his judgment and his lessons from God goes back to the miracle play of the Middle Ages, to the baroque *Schulstück* ("educational play"), to the Jesuit drama, to the clerical didactic plays of Calderón, the *autos sacramentales*. Brecht revived and adapted this sort of play. Exactly what models that old indestructible Augsburg Protestant Brecht used here, consciously or more probably unconsciously, might have been pinpointed by Brecht's teacher Arthur Kutscher who was a scholar of baroque plays, and especially of those of southern Germany.

Like the baroque plays, the *Baden-Baden Cantata* is a thoroughly allegorical drama. The Lord and the chorus of angels have been replaced by the "trained chorus" of the (alleged) Marxists; the "fallen mechanics" represent man, that is, the dying creature who is allowed to enter heaven because he has humbled himself after appropriate clerical instruction and because he has "consented" to the doctrines of humility and salvation. The Sinner, however, condemned for eternity, is the fallen pilot, the bourgeois Charles Nungesser, who persists in arrogance and therefore is doomed. So closely does Brecht follow his models that he even retains the "comic figure" of the clown who, in a grotesquely chilling interlude, repeats the play's thesis in threefold caricature: man is thoroughly evil, thoroughly doomed by original sin, and in need of clerical enlightenment and divine grace, so he can rise to a higher, purer self—the socialized self, the mass self.

Here we have Brecht taking a purely theological work and, with a flick of the wrist, changing it into socialist, quasi-revolutionary propaganda. Church is church, and dogma is dogma, for Marxism as well as for the church, and switching from the one to the other is easy—perhaps not for everybody, but certainly for Brecht.

In another didactic play, *The Measures Taken,* Brecht unfolded the spectrum of Jesuit Machiavellianism. In the *Baden-Baden Cantata,* however, Brecht appropriated the entire doctrine of grace and put it to work for the Party. It is a unique experiment, but the Party undoubtedly would agree with the judgment that basically it failed. Yet, it was certainly Brecht's most important experiment.

I should like to venture a possibility here. Brecht's circle of friends included Walter Benjamin who, if I am not mistaken, also wrote a commentary to the *Baden-Baden Cantata*. Benjamin, who later committed suicide fleeing the Gestapo, was a remarkable person and, along with Rudolf Kassner, probably the most distinguished German essayist of the period. His knowledge of the clerical and secular baroque plays was extraordinary, as shown by his magnificent work on that subject, and this means, of course, that he also had studied scholasticism and theology.

On the surface, Benjamin was a Marxist and Hegelian. But one can see from his fine essays how theological thoughts permeated and colored his Marxist Hegelianism. Undoubtedly, he thought it possible to synthesize, to some extent, Marxism and theological thoughts (even though atheistically garbed). I suspect that he, as no one else, influenced Brecht's strange theological-Marxist didactic play.

On the face of it, it is structured like a miracle play or a didactic clerical play. To recount the historical events, the death of the transoceanic pilot Nungesser, would not help to clarify the play. After Brecht's first naïve dialectic play about Lindbergh's flight, the poet continued to be preoccupied with the theme of transoceanic flying. Nungesser was one of those unfortunates who paid for the experiment with his life.

At the beginning of the play, we see Nungesser and his three mechanics dying after their crash.

They beg for cushions and also for water to quench their thirst. Both are readily available, but what they so desperately long for is not easily granted them. Rather, the "trained chorus" turns to the "masses" first and asks:

Listen! Four men
beg of you to help them.
They have taken to the air and
have fallen to the ground and
do not want to die.
Therefore they beg of you
to help them.
Here we have a cup of water and
a cushion.
You, then, tell us
whether we shall help them.

THE MASSES ANSWERING THE CHORUS: Yes.

THE CHORUS TO THE MASSES: Did they help you?

THE MASSES: No.

THE SPEAKER ADDRESSING THE MASSES: While these men die, it will be investigated whether it is customary for man to help man.

It is now shown that all the advances in technology and natural sciences, all the inventions and discoveries, have not prevented men (in the capitalistic economy) from killing other men and letting them die helplessly. This is shown first by photographs that are passed around, and then by that sadistic knockabout interlude with the three clowns that sparked the scandal in Baden-Baden.

Therefore the following conclusion is reached:

THE MASSES SHOUTING: Man does not help man!

THE LEADER OF THE TRAINED CHORUS: Shall we tear up the cushion?

THE MASSES: Yes.

THE LEADER: Shall we pour away the water?

THE MASSES: Yes.

Thus, the fallen fliers have to die helplessly, without water and without cushions, while the chorus and the masses stand around them. Individual help is wrong. What is needed is the destruction of "power"; that is, in the words of Lenin, the abolition of the class state. Then, individual aid will no longer be necessary.

As long as power rules, help can be denied,
when power no longer rules, help is no longer necessary.
Therefore you should not cry for aid, but abolish power.
Aid and power make up a whole
and the whole must be changed.

The dying men do not get help but "instructions on how to live a blessed life." They are advised to shrink, make themselves as small as possible, to become nothings. They are to humble themselves and to declare their willingness to die. Then they are interrogated:

The Trained Chorus Interrogates the Fallen Fliers While the Masses Watch:

THE TRAINED CHORUS: How high did you fly?

THE THREE FALLEN MECHANICS: We flew extremely high.

THE TRAINED CHORUS: How high did you fly?

THE FALLEN MECHANICS: We flew 12,000 feet high.

THE TRAINED CHORUS: How high did you fly?

THE FALLEN MECHANICS: We flew fairly high.

THE TRAINED CHORUS: How high did you fly?

THE FALLEN MECHANICS: We rose somewhat above the ground.

THE LEADER OF THE TRAINED CHORUS: *(Turns to the Masses)* They rose somewhat above the ground.

THE TRAINED CHORUS: Were you praised?

THE FALLEN MECHANICS: We were not praised enough.

THE TRAINED CHORUS: Were you praised?

THE FALLEN MECHANICS: We were praised.

THE TRAINED CHORUS: Were you praised?

THE FALLEN MECHANICS: We were sufficiently praised.

THE TRAINED CHORUS: Were you praised?

THE FALLEN MECHANICS: We were enormously praised.

THE LEADER OF THE TRAINED CHORUS: *(To the Masses)* They were enormously praised.

THE TRAINED CHORUS: Who are you?

THE FALLEN MECHANICS: We are those who flew across the ocean.

THE TRAINED CHORUS: Who are you?

THE FALLEN MECHANICS: We are some of you.

THE TRAINED CHORUS: Who are you?

THE FALLEN MECHANICS: We are nobody.

THE LEADER OF THE TRAINED CHORUS: *(To the Masses)* They are nobody.

THE TRAINED CHORUS: Who, then, would be dying if you die?

THE FALLEN MECHANICS: Nobody.

They pass the interrogation on the subject of death, while the pilot Nungesser, the individualist, flunks the test and sinks into nothingness. They die but their death is their transfiguration, their resurrection:

The Trained Chorus Addresses the Three Fallen Mechanics:
But you who consent to the flow of things, you do not sink back into nothingness.
You do not dissolve like salt in the water but rise,
dying your death, as you
worked your work,
radically changing radical change.
Dying, then, as you are,
do not acknowledge death.
But accept our command
to rebuild your airplane.
Begin!
In order to fly for us
to the place where we need you,
and at the time when it is necessary. For
we command you
to march with us and to change with us not only
the law of the earth but
the basic law.
Consent that everything is to be changed:
the world and mankind,
and above all the disorder
of the classes of man, because there are two classes of man:
the exploiters and the ignoramuses.

THE FALLEN MECHANICS: We consent to the change.

THE TRAINED CHORUS: When you have improved the world by completing truth, then complete the completed truth. Abandon it!

THE LEADER OF THE TRAINED CHORUS: March!

THE TRAINED CHORUS: Change the world! Change yourselves! Abandon it!

THE LEADER OF THE TRAINED CHORUS: March!

One may well say that Brecht never was closer to his better self and farther from Marxism than here. The play is thoroughly opposed to enlightenment, as is proper for a courageous, honest, cynical pessimist. To be sure, the play teaches a vaguely revolutionary lesson, but it teaches it purely as revelation, as a priestly pronouncement, closely tied to the conceptual and revelational world of the Catholic church—intertwined with the experience of death, grace, last judgment, and resurrection. Not the content of the doctrine is important here, but rather its form, its manner of pronouncement. And this must dismay all Marxists with instinct, if such exist, and delight all theologians with instinct, of whom some existed at the time. For many years afterwards Brecht remained fascinated by the concept of the Last Judgment; even in the last period of his life it influenced the didactic play, *Das Verhör des Lukullus (The Trial of Lucullus).*

Marxism is an acquired doctrine—taught and learned, not revealed; it has nothing to do with death and resurrection. Therefore, *The Baden-Baden Cantata* is essentially a theological and not a Marxist work. If it is to be compared with any-

thing, then with the didactic Catholic plays by
Calderón or Paul Claudel.

Here is a logical place to discuss the entire
subject of the didactic plays. *Der Ozeanflug (The
Flight of the Lindberghs)* is a preparatory study
for *The Baden-Baden Cantata*. It is allegedly written for children and, among other things, teaches
Brecht's atheism at a time when Stalinism considered atheistic propaganda important—and before
Stalin discovered that a godlike dictator can hardly
survive without the framework of a faith in God.
*Die Horatier und die Kuriatier (The Horatii and the
Curiatii)* is a cleverly constructed play for children
which, however, probably would bore an audience
of children. But it does show us the diligent high-
school student Bert Brecht, the industrious Latin
scholar, who is also evident in many passages else-
where in his works.

But the truly important counterpart of *The
Baden-Baden Cantata* is *The Measures Taken*.
Theologically, or perhaps one should say morally
and theologically, it is patterned not after a Marxist
codex but directly after the order rules of St. Igna-
tius of Loyola. The global scope of Jesuit propaganda, admirable in its own way, is spread out before us in the doctrine of self-annihilation—the obliteration of one's own face for the higher glory of
the doctrine. Here is the ceremonial "wiping out of
the face" of the agitators in China:

THE CHIEF OF THE PARTY HEADQUARTERS: You must not
be seen.

THE TWO AGITATORS: We will not be seen.

THE CHIEF OF THE PARTY HEADQUARTERS: If someone gets hurt, he must never be found.

THE TWO AGITATORS: He will never be found.

THE CHIEF OF THE PARTY HEADQUARTERS: Then you are ready to die and to hide the dead man?

THE TWO AGITATORS: We are.

THE CHIEF OF THE PARTY HEADQUARTERS: Then you are no longer yourselves: you are no longer Karl Schmidt of Berlin, you are no longer Anna Kjersk of Kazan, and you are no longer Peter Savich of Moscow, but you are all without names and mothers, empty sheets upon which the revolution writes its instructions.

THE TWO AGITATORS: We are.

THE CHIEF OF THE PARTY HEADQUARTERS: *(hands masks to them, which they put on):*   Then from this hour you are no longer Nobodies, but rather from this hour and probably until your disappearance you are unknown workers, fighters, Chinese, born of Chinese mothers, with yellow skin, speaking Chinese in sleep and delirium.

THE TWO AGITATORS: We are.

Even the actual turningpoint is strictly Jesuit, to a baffling extent. The young comrade fails because he is not willing to join the ruling class, the capitalists, by disguising himself as a useful advisor and toady—just as it had been the practice of the Jesuit Order during the feudal era to ask the friars to prove themselves by acting as courtiers and court officials of the absolute monarchs, particularly in the East. The donning of masks, the obliteration of the face, the costume, the conforming to a situation and a country, the negation of one's true self for the sake of doctrine—all these Bert Brecht did not learn from Marx, but rather from the Jesuit father Baltasar Gracian in his advice to the courtier in *Oráculo,* written in 1647.

The Measures Taken was first performed December 10, 1930, by three "proletarian choruses," with actor Alexander Granach and actress Helene Weigel. With its praise of the Soviet Union and of absolute obedience, *The Measures Taken* was the first of Brecht's plays to receive the seal of approval by the Stalinist party and was generally regarded as a creation strictly for Communist party purposes. Here, Brecht committed himself to the Party body and soul, win or lose, and in particular to its Machiavellian politics, which nine years later required its members to fight for Hitler against the Western democracies. This radical defense of Machiavellianism, this uncompromising rejection of the revolutionary spirit, convictions, and enthusiasm which we find in Brecht's didactic plays might be called the creation of a poet—in the sense that it prophetically anticipates the change, at the hands of Stalin, from a revolutionary party to a robotlike international slave state. From then on, the slogan "Defend the USSR " was the principal slogan of the Party. Such ideological-Machiavellian spadework, like that performed by Brecht, did much to undermine the sound instincts of the revolutionary masses. It enabled Stalin to risk an alliance with Hitler, substantially contributing to Hitler's victory over an internally divided France, without having to worry about the possibility that enough independent revolutionary thinking or feeling men had remained in the Party to attack him and his criminal plans. To this extent *The Measures Taken* is a prologue to the tragic events of 1940 and 1941 from which Hitler, with Stalin's help, almost emerged as victor in the Second World War. The deep anti-revolutionary form of the play was stronger than its pseudo-revolutionary content. After 1945 Brecht prohibited all further performances of *The Measures Taken*, perhaps because of a growing recognition that the deep secrets of one's soul should not be easily surrendered.

During two different phases of Brecht's development and his move toward the Communist party, *The Baden-Baden Cantata of Acquiescence* and *The Measures Taken* are the keys to almost all his later plays: to all, that is, except those where Brecht freed himself from the Party ideology and his own strange atheistic theology and allowed his genius to reign supreme—primarily his masterful *Mother Courage*, *Leben des Galilei (Galileo)*, and also his luscious, thoroughly vivid comedy *Herr Puntila und sein Knecht Matti (Herr Puntilla and His Man Matti)*. These plays do not follow the "general line" of his works which led Brecht deeper and deeper into the propaganda of orthodox Stalinism with its stultifying and mind-paralyzing dictates.

Brecht's general line prominently includes the extensive bulk of his theoretical and dramaturgical writings, which aroused such high hopes in us all, but which later, with their absurd dogmatism, became like a ball and chain, hindering his progress.

Brecht's theory of a non-Aristotelian dramaturgy is analogous to Riemann's and Einstein's non-Euclidean geometry. Brecht seemed to develop new dramaturgical possibilities from Marxism. The Marxist drama was not only to spread Marxist propaganda, but also to create new art forms.

Marx himself had shown little interest in literary problems, although he had literary taste. While working on *Das Kapital* in the famous domed room of the British Museum, he showed interest primarily in the Greek and Latin erotic poets. He loved and admired Heinrich Heine with the infallible instinct of one genius recognizing another, and forgave Heine all seemingly "reactionary" escapades. The fact is—let us not delude ourselves—that Heine's work was inspired not only by the inevitable expectation of the "great revolution," the socialist revolution, but also by his panic fear of it. Heine was not only a poet, perhaps a great poet, but he was above all the greatest prophet of his, and our own, time. He even foresaw and feared Walter Ulbricht as the ultimate outcome of the social revolution—the Philistines emerging as the real victors in the fight for social freedom.

Marx's friend Engels, too, had only limited literary interests. He produced some critical writings on poetry and literature but only a devoted, orthodox Marxist will find them significant.

Brecht, however, saw here an opportunity to study dialectical materialism, with a view to replacing the old forms of dramatic expressionism, as they existed around 1930, with new ones.

In the USSR the so-called *Proletkult* had clearly made a false start. Only the movies, under the genius Eisenstein—primarily with his masterpiece *Potemkin,* but also with his later works—were convincing as new revolutionary art. The Eisenstein tradition was carried on by Pudovkin in his movie *The Mother* which inspired Brecht's own adaptation of Gorki's novel *The Mother.*

What we expected of Bert Brecht and his numerous theoretical discussions was that he would continue the Eisenstein tradition and write the great, sweeping, revolutionary drama, and become a new and greater Büchner.

This, however, was not what Bert Brecht was, not any longer. In no way was he able to hold or continue the level of *Baal* and the *Manual of Piety.* A fanatical hatred for the enthusiasm of the audience had taken possession of this sadistic masochist —an enthusiasm which, to be sure, was denied him for a time after *The Threepenny Opera.* The schoolmaster had finally won. The audience was to be informed and educated, especially about the various twists of the Party line. Enthusiasm was out. Thus he would have been the ideal court poet of the Moscow "Directoire,"which had established itself with the final victory of Stalin over his opponents, Trotsky, above all.

He would have been, that is, if Stalin had not
been and had not always remained a barely civi-
lized tribal chief from the Caucasus whose attention, in good old eastern fashion, was mostly focused
(except for the Moscow ballet) on murdering all
known, presumed, potential, and imagined opponents; however, Stalin showed no great interest in
the modest subtleties of his most obedient court
poet Bert Brecht. Had Stalin been interested, Brecht
might have developed enormously after taking up
residence in Berlin.

But Bert Brecht was by no means written off
in capitalist Berlin. He could have made a second
start there. Although the theater public of Berlin-
West was the most merciless and opinionated in the
world, it was also the freest and most considerate.
Brecht, however, until 1933 kept himself involved
with Party's worker choruses and Agitprop groups,
and produced nothing but theoretical writings
which were not supposed to have any immediate,
human effect, no deeper involvement of the audience—only instruction, only information, nothing
but didactic plays. That's what came of our hope
for a new, enthusiastic, revolutionary drama in the
style of Eisenstein's splendid *Potemkin*.

All we got to see, then—we, the ordinary, non-
Party audience—was *The Mother* at the *Theater
am Schiffbauerdamm*. And here began the great,
lifelong part played by the actress Helene Weigel
who had become Brecht's companion. With grace,
charm, and good humor, and not without coquetry,

she played the role of the mother for which she was much too young at that time.

Later, in exile, Brecht described that performance at the *Theater am Schiffbauerdamm* in a poetic report to the workers' theater of the "Theatre Union," in New York:

Thus we produced the play as a report about great times,
no less golden in the lights of many lamps than the
royal plays produced in earlier days,
no less merry and amusing, yet measured
in the tragic aspects. The players stepped
before the clean curtain, simply and with the characteristic
gestures of their scenes, rendering their lines
in precise, traditional words. The effect of every sentence
was awaited and observed. We waited
until the audience had placed the lines on the scales—we
      often noted
how the deprived, the often cheated
bites the coin with his teeth to see if it is genuine.
Our audience, deprived and often cheated,
should be able to test the lines of the players,
just like a coin. Few props
indicated the scenery. A few tables and chairs—
the indispensable was sufficient. But the photographs
of the great opponents were projected onto the screen in
      the background.
And the words of the socialist classics
painted on strips of cloth or projected onto the screens,
      surrounded
by diligent players. Their appearance was natural.
However, meaningless pages were eliminated in
well-considered condensation. The musical pieces
were lightly presented, with grace. There was much laugh-
      ing

in the audience. The inexhaustible
good humor of the crafty Vlassova, drawn from the con-
    fidence
of her youthful class, produced
happy laughter in the benches of the workers.
They eagerly took advantage of the rare opportunity
to participate, without grave danger, in familiar events, and
    thus
to study them in leisure, and to formulate their own
conduct.

Just where this production "before the workers" took place, I do not know. The *Theater am
Schiffbauerdamm* was not patronized by "proletar-
ians," except for a few bohemians from the Ro-
manische Café. But the production was a great success, just as Brecht later described it, because of the
spirited, measured and joyous atmosphere, and the
grace and subtle coquetry of the charming yet
tough Helene Weigel who then and there became
the authentic Bert Brecht interpreter.

Unfortunately Brecht, with unshakable tenac-
ity, continued to pursue the pattern of the didactic
play. The fanaticism of the convert held him in its
grip; to him, the most important dogma seemed to
be: "I believe because it is absurd." His only goal
was the direct, primitive, merciless, pedantic Party
propaganda. Inescapably he seemed to become
the victim of his own intellect, of his own sensitiv-
ity, almost of his own talent. He evidently would
have best liked to write only for the propagandists,
to the exclusion of the bourgeois public.

It is doubtful whether the Party fully appreciated this sacrifice—not just the German Party but the Party in general. The Party had plenty of mediocre Agitprop writers. Johannes R. Becher, a genuine poet, had just turned into one—and one of the most insipid. What the Party undoubtedly expected were run-of-the-mill dramatists who would be able to convert the nonbelievers, that is, the sophisticated, leftist Berlin bourgeois public and the nonfanatical workers. But Brecht held firmly to his formula, and also to his theological hue. His world remains theologically divided—into judges *(judex ergo cum sedebit)* and poor mortals *(quid sum miser tunc dicturus?).* On one occasion, these judges are called "control chorus." In *The Trial of Lucullus,* his last didactic play, they are the Judges of the Dead.

Only once, in this period, did Brecht write a normally constructed, politically oriented play, and it was a very effective one: *Die Gewehre der Frau Carrar (Señora Carrar's Rifles),* a story from the Spanish Civil War, modeled after a drama by the distinguished Irish author J. M. Synge.

Otherwise, the path of his "alienated" theater leads to the primitive puppet show or to the *commedia dell'arte,* as in the case of the overrated *The Good Woman of Setzuan.* One could make a case for saying that Brecht, for some reason—perhaps bordering on the pathological—was systematically choking off his dramatic talent after the time of his failures.

When Brecht saw the Reichstag burning, he

knew, with good reason, that he had to leave Germany immediately. He gathered a small group of his associates about him. They first went to Prague, a main route for emigrants leaving for the West.

The Czechoslovak atmosphere was hardly beneficial for him. Was Brecht at all receptive to the atmosphere of a country and its characteristic national traits? The comedy *Schwejk im zweiten Weltkrieg (Schweyk in the Second World War)* does have some humorous folkloristic features, but it misses almost entirely the character of the "good soldier Schweyk" which by then had already become a classic. Brecht's Schweyk does have the broad goodnaturedness of the original, but lacks his stubborn pigheadedness. The farce seems to belong more to the milieu of the popular stage in Munich, which Brecht knew well, than to that of the Czech stage. The second work, written during this time, *The Threepenny Novel,* which lampoons Bat'a or at least the system of the Bat'a works, is—as mentioned before—a concoction lacking humor and imagination.

But in general the years of exile were Brecht's best creative years because in foreign countries he was able, time and again, to shake off the orthodoxy of the Party. In 1938 he published the sharply pointed dramatic pamphlet *Furcht und Elend des Dritten Reiches (The Private Life of the Master Race),* a series of twenty-four dramatic scenes, each of which makes its satirical point with astonishing precision—as though Brecht himself had experienced the terror, despair, tension, cowardice, and blustering, as well as the specific kind of humaneness and silent heroism of the day-to-day life in the *Third Reich.* A work like this—alive, relevant, yet put together merely from more or less unreliable oral reports, rumors, and newspaper clippings—does show that Brecht was indeed a poet and a dramatist.

It is characteristic of Brecht that he could shape ideas magnificently and with the hand of a real artist, and then again fashion the same ideas clumsily, lifelessly, and completely falsely when the twisted orthodoxy and the intellectualism of the little Marxist schoolteacher took hold of him. He wrote another piece about Hitlerism, an allegorical play, *Die Rundköpfe und die Spitzköpfe (The Round Heads and the Peaked Heads)*—hopelessly discrediting not only himself as a Marxist teacher, but Marxist teaching in general. Writing with the stubborness of the primitive class-war theoretician, and in the abstract homily style of his didactic plays, he propounded a hypothesis about the Hitler Reich that went somewhat like this: Racist theory and anti-Semitism are only window dressing for Hitler's game. Here, as everywhere else, class war is at the root of it all. Hitler will somehow come to terms with the rich Jews, the Hindenburg regime will return in some form or other, the rich—Christians and Jews alike—will sit at the table of plenty while the poor and the workers will be oppressed as they always have been. Even racism is nothing but a weapon in the class struggle of the bourgeoisie against the working class. Thus spoke Brecht in 1934 and 1935.

This was the gospel according to Marx, but it also turned out to be disastrously wrong; Europe's Jews, rich and poor, who could not flee, were wiped out by Hitler almost to the last man, woman, and child. This was completely un-Marxian, because the Marxists saw Hitler only as the exponent of industry and finance pushing for a war with Russia, the land of the workers. Unfortunately, Hitler on this point did not follow the rules set up for him by Marxism. Thereupon the Marxist theory was "corrected" and Stalin entered his honorably intended alliance with Hitler. As a side effect, five million Jews met their deaths, which did not bother Stalin much but which ought to have had some effect on Bert Brecht—causing him, at least, to remain silent.

All wrong. In 1935, it may have been excusable to publish such madness as *The Round Heads and the Peaked Heads;* but for Brecht to include that same piece in 1955 in his collected works rather than shamefacedly bury it in deep oblivion, as he wisely did with other works, demonstrates the callous, brutal cynicism of the tender-hearted, lovable poet, as he was eulogized after his death in 1956 by his friends and associates in many obituaries. It was Mack the Knife's cynicism to the highest degree.

In the same manner as Brecht, after 1928, repeatedly had tried to lift *The Threepenny Opera* to the level of twentieth-century class warfare, so he tried in 1941–1942 to do the reverse: to reduce, in the didactic play, *Der aufhaltsame Aufstieg des Arturo Ui (The Resistible Ascent of Arturo Ui)*, the beginning of the Hitler regime and the march into Austria to the level of a Chicago gangster drama. We are familiar with Brecht's romantic predilection for that type of outdated gangster movie and trashy novel, which decades before had inspired him to the worst of his early plays. Brecht's most ridiculous pose, perhaps, is his antiquated romanticism, his romantic quiet love of demonic gangsters, boxers, prizefighters, racing drivers, and similar representatives of culture, which gave him, as Rimbaud before him, the excuse to despise poetry as an avocation. Rimbaud actually renounced poetry. At least he proved his beliefs by his actions. He really became a gangster, an arms profiteer, a secret slave trader in Abyssinia in the pay of a highly questionable company in Aden, traces of which—as I happen to know—still existed after 1939. Bert Brecht, too, in romantic self-delusion, might have dreamed of such a career. Yet, he remained a Berlin man of letters as long as he lived. The gangster play of *The Resistible Ascent of Arturo Ui* is a pitiful failure. It is not such a dangerous literary and ideological disaster as *The Round Heads and the Peaked Heads*— it simply is a failure. An antiquated gangster play in the style of 1910 and 1920 cannot possibly convey the vaguest notion of the satanic phenomenon of Hitler and his henchmen. Brecht's romantic-

didactic prettification is almost a stroke in favor of,
not against, Hitler.

Such contradictions are always to be expected
in Brecht. He was not the experimenter he fancied
himself to be, and which he kept assuring us he
was, in the volumes of his old and new *Experiments.* Essentially, he was simply a stubborn Bavarian who never yielded to criticism unless it was
backed by a firm power that could threaten him.
Then, to be sure, he showed very different traits.
But in the democratic countries where he lived
after 1933, no such dangerous power existed—or at
most only in one form: the failure of his plays. Such
failure, however, was his fate during his exile.

Yet, on the whole, these emigration years in
the Western democratic countries, where the fist of
the Party did not threaten him daily and hourly,
were the most productive of his life since the time
of *The Threepenny Opera.* In 1939, he finished his
most mature and beautiful drama, *Mother Courage,*
which was first performed in an excellent production in Zürich. In 1940, in Finland, he worked on
the truly merry, sensuously enjoyable, delightful
folk drama, *Herr Puntila and His Man Matti.* Unfortunately, that play was again the subject of one
of those painful affairs that occurred from time to
time in his life. Brecht, the master at collective
authorship who never failed to acknowledge the
lowliest of his assistants in book editions, forgot to
mention that he owed the story and even the dramatic outline of *Puntila* to his Finnish hostess, the

poet Hella Wuolijoki. He added her name only later. The first performance did not take place until 1948, in the Zürich *Schauspielhaus*.

In 1937–1938 he worked on *Galileo* which, in its dramatic conception, is just as free, beautiful, and self-assured as *Mother Courage*. But it contains dry, bony, doctrinaire passages. The powerful final dialogue between Galileo and his favorite student Andrea Sarti, with its sudden dramatic turn, is in the best style of the much-despised Ibsen. Missing, however, is the masterly balance and interrelationship between problem and dramatic action which make *A Doll's House* or *Ghosts* lastingly effective plays despite their antiquated themes. Time and again Brecht breaks his dramatic power and veers toward the abstract didactic play—but this time he takes the precaution of teaching the liberal bourgeois progressive message, without an explicit Communist conclusion.

Galileo was Brecht's big chance in the United States. The producer, Joseph Losey, wanted to stage the drama in grand style at the Coronet Theater in Hollywood, starring the inspired actor Charles Laughton, a truly ideal interpreter for the part of Galileo. Money was plentiful. Brecht himself could rehearse the work for more than a year. Yet, the production was not successful. As the director, he relentlessly worked for the "alienation effect"—the motivating force of the play was to be not emotion, but instruction of the audience. This instruction—the theme in Ibsen's sense—was, to be sure, devastatingly topical at the time of the opening night.

The play presents Galileo as the scientific genius whose great love of discovery and truth does not lead him to promote progress for mankind in general, but rather separates him and shuts him out. Under the pressure of outside influences his research, as far as its use in society is concerned, becomes abstract; it can be used both for the benefit and for the destruction of mankind. Galileo himself realizes this in the end and acknowledges it in the big final dialogue with his student Andrea: this is Galileo's guilt and tragedy.

One senses what Brecht ultimately intended to say. Indeed, he said it himself in his "Concluding Comments" about the American premiere: "It must be remembered that our production took place at the time and in the land where the atom bomb had just been created and used militarily, and where nuclear physics was shrouded in deep secrecy. The day the bomb was dropped will be hard to forget for anyone who at the time lived in the United States. The war with Japan had caused real hardship in the United States. The troop transports left from the West Coast, and there the wounded and the victims of Asiatic diseases returned. When the first newspaper reports reached Los Angeles, it was clear that the bomb meant the end of this fearful war, and the return of sons and brothers. But the large metropolis was mourning, and expressed its sadness in an amazing way. The writer of this play heard bus drivers and saleswomen in the fruit markets voice nothing but shock. It was a victory, but it held all the shame of defeat. Then the military and the politicians cloaked the awesome energy source into secrecy, which irritated the intellectuals. The freedom of research, mutual exchange of discoveries, the international brotherhood of the scientists were paralyzed by authorities who were strongly distrusted. Distinguished physicists fled the services of their bellicose government; one of the most famous accepted a teaching post which obliged him to waste his time teaching at a very low level, only to avoid having to work for the government. It had become shameful to make a discovery."

And, coming back to *Galileo,* Brecht concluded: "Galileo's crime might be regarded as the original sin of science. He made a sharply defined specialized science out of astronomy which deeply interested a new class, the bourgeoisie, because it abetted the revolutionary social trends of that age."

This is the real crime of *Galileo,* and not the oppression of free inquiry by the church. The Communist Bert Brecht specifically forbids the church's part in the trial of Galileo to be caricatured on the stage.

There is something impressive about the consistency with which Brecht, as a director, insisted on his interpretation which eventually spoiled his success. In his later comments he does not exactly exclude the possibility of staging the play simply as a historical drama; he only says that such a staging would make the drama more difficult to understand.

Brecht—who during his exile had lived (often under conditions of great privation) in Czechoslovakia, Austria, Denmark, Sweden, Finland, France, and England and who finally had arrived in Hollywood—was satisfied to make a living by working on movies that could hardly have interested him. Thus he wrote a script for the tenor Richard Tauber, after Leoncavallo's *Pagliacci*. Nor did he reject an occasional dramaturgical routine assignment. For instance, he adapted Gerhart Hauptmann's *Biberpelz (Beaver Coat)* and its sequel *Der rote Hahn (The Red Rooster)* into one single play—not a bad idea at that. Another time, upon the suggestion of director Bernhard Reich, he adapted the last two acts of *Camille*, by the younger Dumas. Brecht presumably considered his work on that movie as a routine assignment; but the American Ernest Bornemann, to whom we are indebted for a valuable biographical sketch of Brecht (published in Peter Heuchel's magazine *Sinn und Form*, 1957, issues 1–3), maintains that the movie bears unmistakably Brechtian traits. The movie, incidentally, was no success either; in fact, it was a failure, although Brecht, together with the director, Slatan Dudow, had produced a significant social film before 1933, *Kuhle Wampe*, and thus had a fair amount of experience in movie making.

Throughout the time of his exile, Brecht wrote antifascist propaganda in the form of verses, songs, and proclamations, which were broadcast by the Allies, especially by the German division of BBC, and which found their way illegally into Germany. Frequently it was not propaganda for humanist democracy. As long as he lived in Europe, it was pure Russian propaganda, bitter propaganda of death. Here are a few verses of this sort, entitled "To the German Soldiers in the East":

On the map in the school atlas
the road to Smolensk is no longer
than the little finger of the Führer, but
on the snowfields it is longer,
very long, too long.

The snow will not last forever, only till spring.
But man will not last forever, either. He will not last
till spring.

Thus I must die, this I know.
In the coat of a bandit I must die,
in the shirt of a larcenist and killer.

As one of the many, as one of the thousands,
chased as a bandit, killed as a killer.

Because I have broken into
the peaceful land of the farmers and workers,
of great organization and unceasing construction,
trampling down and crushing with my wheels the grain
    and farmsteads,
to pillage the workshops, the mills, the dams,
to disrupt instruction in a thousand schools,
to disturb the councils of the tireless soviets:
For this I now must die like a rat
cornered by a farmer.

So that the face of the earth
will be cleansed of me,

the leper! So that an example can be set
of me, for all times, on how to treat
bandits, killers,
and the flunkies of bandits and killers.

Between 1944 and 1947, the latter being the
year of Brecht's return to Europe, he wrote *The
Caucasian Chalk Circle.* It is an epic drama, somewhat wordy, about the legend of the loyal maid
who rescues the child of her mistress and adopts
it—a variant of the Chinese legend of the chalk
circle that previously had been adapted by Klabund. Klabund had written the play for his consort
Carola Neher; later it became a great stage success,
primarily because of Elisabeth Bergner. Brecht's
play has little in common with Klabund's stage version aside from its basic theme. The play, unquestionably, has magnificent and moving passages—
they constitute a heresy against Brecht's prescrip-
tion of alienation. Such heresies almost became the
rule during Brecht's stay in the United States; if
Brecht had remained there longer, he may have
become more traditional and undoubtedly a great
playwright. Some primitive Soviet propaganda,
presumably written long after completion of *The
Caucasian Chalk Circle,* was tacked on to the play
as a prologue and has nothing to do with the plot.

In 1945, jointly with Lion Feuchtwanger,
Brecht wrote *The Visions of Simone Machard,* a
play about Joan of Arc, the maid of Orleans, Vol-
taire's *Pucelle,* and G. B. Shaw's *Saint Joan.*

Brecht's and Feuchtwanger's story portrays a

little French girl who, after Hitler's invasion of France, has visions in which she identifies herself with Saint Joan, and the people around her with the followers or enemies of Joan of Arc. It presents, as it were, Joan of Arc as the patron saint of the resistance movement against the Germans—tailored, perhaps, for a stage performance in Paris. The strictly anti-British tinge of several scenes more or less follows the de Gaulle line.

This was the second time Brecht used the Joan of Arc theme. His first treatment, *Saint Joan of the Stockyards,* written in 1929 and 1930 and placed in a childishly conceived milieu of Chicago profiteers, was partly a parody of Schiller and Shakespeare, partly a Communist-line didactic play. It was an odd, at times grotesque work, in many ways monumental and impressive, but on the whole stillborn. A third version of the Saint Joan theme followed later in Berlin.

In 1945, the end of Brecht's time in exile approached. Like so many of us he had somehow pulled through. Like most intellectuals, he was modest in his personal needs. He paid little attention to his surroundings, as long as he had a room in which to pace up and down undisturbed and think, and a table for writing. His mobility during exile was hampered only by the stack of newspaper clippings which grew higher by the day and without which he could not—or thought he could not—carry on. All his life he was a tireless newspaper and magazine reader; he needed and used factual material and had to have it handy.

He packed his things for his return to Europe, after swearing an oath to the United States authorities that he had never been a member of the Communist party—an oath amusing to those in the know, although it was probably no perjury.

His return was carefully organized, with all the tactical, diplomatic, and—in a remoter sense—commercial shrewdness that characterized him.

He first went to Zürich, whose Schauspielhaus had never deserted him. There he directed *Antigone*. From there he moved his residence to Vienna, a good listening post and a little closer to his real destination, Berlin.

Then something unexpected happened: The newspapers reported that he had become an Austrian citizen. How long he kept that status, I do not know—presumably until long after his fame became established as the official, celebrated playwright of the "German Democratic Republic" and of East Berlin. Perhaps until his death. His complex motivations were often impenetrable. There was talk about his taking over the direction of the Salzburg Festivals. *Totentanz (Dance of Death)*, of which only fragments exist, reads like a woodcut turned into a play and was meant to take the place of Hofmannsthal's *Jedermann (Everyman)*. But nothing came of it. East Berlin got in touch with Brecht through the poet and minister Johannes R. Becher. Preliminary negotiations began with Pieck,

Becher, and the entire political administration of the then Russian zone.

Brecht aimed high—as high as had Richard Wagner. The latter had asked King Ludwig II of Bavaria for a theater of his own, in Munich or Bayreuth, where he could produce his "music drama of the future" entirely as he saw fit. Similarly, Bert Brecht asked Pieck and Ulbricht for the old *Theater am Schiffbauerdamm* where *The Threepenny Opera* had had its never-ending run. Brecht wanted to use it entirely at his discretion, so that he could direct his drama of the future—the epic, alienated theater—in every detail and exactly as he wished, independent of commercial success or failure. All this was promised to him if he would move his residence to East Berlin. Those who gave the promise kept it to the dot: They accepted the entire commercial risk. The Berlin Ensemble at the *Theater am Schiffbauerdamm,* was and probably still is, fully subsidized by the government.

King Ludwig never had granted that much to his fanatically adored Wagner. The Bayreuth enterprise was financially a network of short-term loans granted by the patron king—a net in which Wagner could be caught at any time and, in fact, was caught. Gnashing his teeth, he had to grant performance rights of *Ring des Nibelungen (Ring of the Nibelung)* to the Royal Opera in Munich immediately after the Bayreuth production because Wagner's operas served as security for Ludwig's treasury. Since Ludwig himself, despite his enthusiasm for Wagner, knew nothing about music, the operas were shown in mediocre performances which Wagner refused to attend. After Wagner's death, Siegfried and Cosima Wagner repaid the Bayreuth loans to the businesslike royal House of Wittelsbach. The royal family made an additional unsavory profit by selling the priceless original scores of Wagner's works—Wagner's personal gift of friendship to King Ludwig—for 800,000 marks to a group of industrialists who later donated them to Adolf Hitler on the occasion of his fiftieth birthday.

Pieck, the old Communist, made no such unkingly deals; he concluded no shabby loan arrangements with Bert Brecht and traded no original *The Threepenny Opera* manuscripts. His government paid what the Berlin Ensemble needed and could not raise.

On the other hand, there was no reason to fear that Brecht, like Richard Wagner, would waste part of the subsidy in extravagant personal expenditures. Brecht needed no palazzo on trips to Palermo or Venice, nor did he need a Villa Wahnfried in East Berlin or Potsdam. All he requested and received for his private use was a relatively modest, comfortable apartment, where he could store his stack of clippings, smoke his cheap black cigars, and drink his bottles of vodka or brandy when he worked.

But Brecht, like Richard Wagner, wanted his own theater. Here, as the reports of his associates show, he worked tirelessly, conscientiously, and meticulously. He directed every play down to the minutest gesture, as if it were a ballet. He gave his actors long, well-thought-out directives, half technical, half Marxist-ideological. To the stage door of his theater were pinned the dates of rehearsals as well as Marxist courses for actors: one without the other seemed unthinkable to him. It certainly seemed unthinkable to the formal manager of the theater, Brecht's wife Helene Weigel. He also trained a crop of new actors.

Richard Wagner had promised to produce in Bayreuth some of the great composers of the past, but he never kept that promise. Brecht did keep a similar promise. He played Molière and the *Sturm und Drang* poet Lenz. Undoubtedly he would have produced Georg Büchner. He adapted these plays in versions of his own, just as he had adapted (unfortunately with not much taste) Sophocles' *Antigone* in Zürich, in the translation by Friedrich Hölderlin, and staged by his loyal friend Caspar Neher.

The Berlin Ensemble at the *Schiffbauerdamm* was the pride of East Berlin, the pride of the German Democratic Republic—and not without cause. Brecht did his best to make himself an official functionary. He missed no opportunity to kowtow to Stalin, Stalinism, and the Stalinist government of East Germany.

He remained the great old man of the theater of the Eastern regime, the only author who could be shown, with some hope of success, in Paris, London, or Milan.

He did not do much creative writing in those
final days. Perhaps his own theater devoured him.
More likely, the atmosphere he liked so much (he
was a born servant, not a ruler) did not challenge
him to creativity as much as the tougher but health-
ier climate of the United States and the other
Western democracies had done. What he now
wrote—*Kalendergeschichten (Calendar Stories)*,
or *Die Geschäfte des Herrn Julius Caesar (The
Private Life of Mr. Julius Caesar)*—were sterile,
dull enlightenment tracts which even contradicted
the spirit of "realistic" Soviet hero worship.

Thus, he wrote a little and directed some plays
until he died. The conversion of the stage into a
alienated puppet theater was a dead end. But a
production such as his *Mother Courage* was magnificent. He remained self-contradictory to the end,
a stubborn man who knew well enough that he
could affect people only if he yielded as a doctrinaire theoretician. He had partly come around to
this, as is attested by notes taken by his assistants
during his last months, when he suddenly died.

And when he died, on August 14, 1956, we all
knew that the man who lay dead had not only been
a grotesque, misled, doctrinaire rebel, but also Germany's only representative playwright, who half of
his life had stubbornly worked against himself, his
dramatic genius, and his genuine, natural appeal to
the public.

6

Postscript
to the Second
German Edition

After Brecht's death, his name quickly became world famous. The English, American, and French articles and books published about him would fill many shelves. The visit of the Berlin Ensemble to the Paris *Théâtre des Nations* was probably the greatest success in the history of that theater since its founding by Sarah Bernhardt.

It was primarily *Mother Courage* and, in the second place, *Galileo* that established and sustained this fame. They are considered *the* classic dramas of our time.

Fame, and especially world fame, is almost always based on misunderstanding, but rarely so tragically as in this instance. These two plays, seen today from our present point in history, deny everything that Brecht had worked for all his life in his dramatic experiments. *Mother Courage* is a thoroughly conservative, sweeping, magnificently composed bourgeois drama—the work of a theatrical genius. In German literature it is close to Gerhart Hauptmann's dramas. *Galileo* has been interpreted in all kinds of ideological terms—as have many of Brecht's works—especially its ending with its long, dramatically unintegrated dialogues. This does not change the fact that *Galileo*, too, is a "modern classic" in a conservative, bourgeois sense. *Mother Courage* and *Galileo* are great plays—I would say, the greatest German plays since Gerhart Hauptmann. They were written during exile in the Western countries; their structure, apart from some ideological curlicues perhaps added at a later date, shows how far Brecht, at that time, had departed from his ideology.

But there is also another, geninue line of which we expected so much and which has become quite apparent through the production of *Saint Joan of the Stockyards* as directed so splendidly by Gustaf Gründgens at the Hamburg *Schauspielhaus,* and also through several interesting posthumous publications in Peter Heuchel's remarkable journal, *Sinn und Form.* Brecht really was striving for something which, in the 1920's, after publication of his *Experiments* we all sensed, knew, and expected: he really wanted to create the great, monumental, heroic drama, reformulated from the elements of dialectical materialism. *Saint Joan* was already a farce trying to deal with this delusion, a ridiculing of the heroic style; it was preceded by early drafts of *Saint Joan,* especially a very revealing one called *Der Brotladen (The Bakery)*—published in *Sinn und Form*—the earliest version of the Saint Joan drama, still presented realistically and in great dramatic style.

Brecht wanted to create this great, new, heroic, materialistic drama. But his fame is based on something different—on something he could only have felt to be a compromise, if he, in fact, was still interested at all, toward the end of his life, in his experimental theories.

What has remained of that part of his work that represents the attainment of his goals—which, in the last analysis, he betrayed? A didactic poem,

meant to enlighten and teach, written in pedantic
hexameters, in the style of Lucretius' *De rerum
natura:* Brecht's attempt to write a didactic poem
about Marx's *Communist Manifesto* in the Lucre-
tian style. Clever fragments of this, composed in
mediocre hexameters, were published in *Sinn und
Form,* 1957. These attempts explicitly acknowledge
that dialectical materialism as a new art form is impossible; and they testify to this failure, just as—at
the other extreme—the success of *Mother Courage*
testifies to it.

Brecht's life and work are tragic. They have an
innate tragedy such as he himself rarely, although
sometimes, was able to present on the stage. And
when we say that his life was tragic, we mean that it
was an eminent, though broken, life. Only eminent
men are destined to have tragic lives.

W. H.

7

Epilogue: Brecht's Literary Estate

Thirty-six volumes of Brecht's collected works have been published in German so far—and more are yet to come. There is also a beautiful Japan-paper edition of eight volumes (each containing 1,000 to 3,000 pages) and a twenty-volume pocket-book edition with the same contents, all published by Suhrkamp. A critical, scientific-historical edition including all available letters, sketches, drafts, diaries is unlikely under present conditions. It would undoubtedly shed light on many dim parts of his life. However, the extant text material, based on the Brecht archives in East Berlin, is abundant.

The longest posthumous publication is the play *Turandot* and the related novel *Tui*—the reflections and the story of the Tuis, a privileged sect of sophists in an imaginary empire in China. Brecht's *Turandot* has only a few features of the simplified main plot in common with the original comedy *Turandot* by the Venetian Grozzi or its adaptation by Friedrich Schiller. The extant fragments, which fill the entire Volume xiv are not developed sufficiently to permit a general picture of the outline and meaning of the play.

In *Turandot,* mention is made several times of the Tuistic School of Lickspittle. Lickspittle poetry of various kinds, addressed to Stalinist Russia, is contained in the three posthumous volumes of verse. They include, for example, an endless hymn to the cultivation of millet in a collective farm of the democratic republic of Kazakhstan; perhaps it was this hymn that earned Brecht the Stalin Prize, and he may have written it for that purpose—I cannot imagine any other. But the three volumes also contain quiet and sensitive poetry, such as the "Buckow Elegies," and courageous verses such as the sharp attack on the political leadership of the German Democratic Republic in the epigram on the Berlin Revolt of June 17. Nothing, though, comes close to the tunes or organ sounds of the earlier *Manual of Piety* or *Baal* poetry.

The outstanding work in the four new volumes of plays is Brecht's final (the third) version of the life and death of Joan of Arc; it is based on a radio drama by Anna Seghers which, in turn, is based on the 1431 trial documents concerned with Joan of Arc. Brecht's *Der Prozess der Jeanne d'Arc zu Rouen 1431 (The Trial of Joan of Arc in Rouen, 1431)* is a plain, strong, effective, historical play, grist for his Berlin Ensemble. It contains no trace of alienation, non-Aristotelian dramaturgy, or other dramatic doctrines of the earlier Brecht.

Producers will be especially interested in Brecht's adaptations of plays by Sophocles, Shakespeare *(Coriolanus)*, Molière *(Don Juan)*, George Farquhar, and Jacob Michael Reinhold Lenz *(Der Hofmeister)*. The most significant of these is the *Coriolanus* adaptation, in which Brecht, without changing much of the wording of the original, actually presents Shakespeare's drama upside down. The other texts were mostly written by Brecht or his closest associates while staging them at the Berlin Ensemble.

Brecht's voluminous posthumously published works, then, offer much of interest and are worth knowing, but there seems to be nothing that would significantly change our image of Brecht. The same will probably be true of the volumes yet to come, unless and until his personal correspondence is published.

W. H.

Hamburg, March 1968

Chronology

1898 (February 10):	Born in Augsburg.
1914–1916:	Freelance theater critic.
1917:	Graduated from Realgymnasium (high school) in Augsburg. Studied natural history and medicine in Munich.
1918:	Medical corpsman in military hospital.
1919:	Continued studies in Munich.
1920:	Dramatic consultant in Munich.
1924:	Moved to Berlin, occasional stage manager under Max Reinhardt.
1926:	*Baal* performed in Vienna (under the aegis of Hugo v. Hofmannsthal).
1927:	*Domestic Breviary* published.
1928–1929:	Attended Marxist School.
1929:	*Das Badener Lehrstück vom Einverständnis* (Baden-Baden).

1930:   *Aufstieg und Fall der Stadt Ma-
                 hagonny* (Leipzig); *Die Maß-
                 nahme* (Berlin); *Die heilige Jo-
                 hanna der Schlachthöfe* com-
                 pleted.

1933:   Flight to Prague, Vienna, Zurich;
                 Denmark (1938); Sweden (1939);
                 Finland (1940).

1935:   Traveled to Moscow.

1936:   *Die Rundköpfe und die Spitz-
                 köpfe* (Copenhagen).

1938:   *Furcht und Elend des Dritten
                 Reiches* (Paris).

1936–1939:   Co-publisher of *Das Wort,* which
                 appeared in Moscow. Also wrote
                 for the German freedom radio
                 station.

1941:   Arrival in the United States. Oc-
                 casional work for movies in Holly-
                 wood. *Mutter Courage und ihre
                 Kinder* (Zurich).

1943:   *Der gute Mensch von Sezuan*
                 (Zurich).

1944–1945:   Wrote *The Caucasian Chalk Cir-
                 cle.*

1948:   First performance of *The Cau-
                 casian Chalk Circle* at Carleton
                 College in Minnesota.
                 *Herr Puntila und sein Knecht
                 Matti* (Zurich). Brecht returns to
                 Germany (East Berlin). *Kleines
                 Organon für das Theater.*

1949:   Established the *Berlin Ensemble*

	with Helene Weigel, his wife, as director. Brecht is a member of the artistic advisory board.
1951:	Won the East German National Prize.
1954:	Won the Stalin Peace Prize. Receives first prize at the International Theater Festival in Paris for his production of *Mutter Courage und ihre Kinder*.
1956 (August 14):	Dies in East Berlin.

Selected
Bibliography

PLAYS

Baal, 1922. English translation, 1963.

Trommeln in der Nacht, 1923; also in *Stücke* 1, 1962. *Drums in the Night*, in *Seven Plays by Bertolt Brecht* [Eric Bentley, editor] 1961.

Im Dickicht der Städte, 1924; also in *Stücke* 1, 1962. *Jungle of Cities* in *Theatre Arts*, vol. 45, Aug. 1961.

Leben Eduards des zweiten von England, (with Lion Feuchtwanger), 1924; also in *Stücke*, 2, 1962.

Mann ist Mann, 1927; also in *Stücke* 2, 1962. *A Man's a Man*, in *Seven Plays by Bertolt Brecht* [Eric Bentley, editor] 1961.

Aufstieg und Fall der Stadt Mahagonny, 1929; also in *Stücke* 1, 1962. *The Rise and Fall of the City Mahagonny*, in brochure with Columbia Records K3L-243

Der Ozeanflug, in *Versuche* 2, 1930–32. *The Flight of the Lindberghs*, Universal Editions, n.d.

Die Dreigroschenoper, in *Versuche* 3, 1930–32; also in *Stücke* 3, 1962. *The Threepenny Opera,* in *From the Modern Repertoire* [Eric Bentley, editor] 1949.

Das Badener Lehrstück vom Einverständnis, in *Versuche* 2, 1930–32; also in *Stücke* 3, 1962. *The Baden-Baden Cantata of Acquiescence,* in *Harvard Advocate* vol. 134, No. 4 (Feb. 1951).

Der Jasager and *Der Neinsager* in *Versuche* 4, 1930–32; also in *Stücke* 4, 1962. *He Who Says Yes* and *He Who Says No* in *Accent,* vol. 2 (Autumn 1946).

Die Maßnahme in *Versuche* vol. 4, 1930–32, also in *Stücke* 4, 1962. *The Measures Taken* in *Colorado Review,* vol. 50, No. 1 (Winter 1956–57).

Die heilige Johanna der Schlachthöfe in *Versuche,* 1932. *Saint Joan of the Stockyards* in *From the Modern Repertoire,* vol. 3, 1956, [Eric Bentley, editor]; also in *Plays by Bertolt Brecht,* Vol. 2, 1962.

The Round Heads and the Peaked Heads, or Rich and Rich Make Good Company in *International Literature* vol. 5, 1937. *Die Rundköpfe und die Spitzköpfe* in *Stücke* 6, 1962.

Señora Carrar's Rifles in *Theatre Workshop* April/June 1938. *Die Gewehre der Frau Carrar,* in *Stücke* 7, 1962.

Das Verhör des Lukullus 1939; also in *Stücke* 7, 1962. *The Trial of Lucullus* 1943.

Mother Courage and Her Children, 1941. *Mutter Courage und ihre Kinder* in *Versuche* 9, 1949–57; also in *Stücke* 7 1962.

Der gute Mensch von Sezuan 1942; also in *Versuche* 12, 1949–57; in *Stücke* 8, 1962. *The Good Woman of Setzuan* in *Parables for the Theatre* [Eric Bentley, editor] 1948.

Leben des Galilei, 1943; also in *Versuche* 14, 1949–57, in *Stücke* 8, 1962. *Galileo,* in *From the Modern Repertoire* II [Eric Bentley, editor] 1952.

Die Gesichte der Simone Marchard, (with Lion Feuchtwanger) 1943, also in *Stücke* 9, 1962. *The Visions of Simone Marchard,* 1961.

Schwejk im zweiten Weltkrieg, 1944; also in *Stücke* 10, 1962.

The Private Life of the Master Race, 1944. *Furcht und Elend des Dritten Reiches* in *Stücke* 6, 1962.

Die Mutter 1946, also in *Stücke* 5, 1962.

The Horatii and the Curiatii in *Accent,* vol. 8, Autumn 1947. *Die Horatier und die Kuriatier* in *Stücke* 5, 1962.

The Caucasian Chalk Circle in *Parables for the Theatre* [Eric Bentley, editor;] 1948.

Die Tage der Commune, 1949; also in *Stücke* 10, 1962.

Herr Puntila und sein Knecht Matti in *Versuche* 10, 1949–57; in *Stücke* 9, 1962. *Herr Puntila and His Man Matti,* Scenes 9 and 11 in *Accent,* vol. 14, No. 2, Spring 1954.

Der kaukasische Kreidekreis in *Sinn und Form,* 1949; also in *Versuche* 13, 1949–57, in *Stücke* 10, 1962.

Die Tage der Commune, 1949; also in *Stücke* 10, 1962.

The Baby Elephant, in *Wake,* vol. 8, Autumn 1949. *Das Elefantenkalb,* in *Stücke* 2, 1962.

The Exception and the Rule in *Chrysalis,* vols. 11–12, 1954. *Die Ausnahme und die Regel* in *Stücke* 5, 1962.

Der aufhaltsame Aufstieg des Arturo Ui, in *Stücke* 9, 1962.

FICTION

Dreigroschenroman, 1934, 1951. Eng., *A Penny for the Poor*, 1937; Am. *Threepenny Novel* 1956.
Kalendergeschichten, 1953; *Geschichten vom Herrn Keuner*, collected edition, 1958. *Meditations of Herr Keuner* in *New Statesman*, Nov. 3, 1956.
Die Geschäfte des Herrn Julius Caesar 1957. *The Private Life of Mr. Julius Caesar* in *Nimbus, New English Review*, vol. 4, Feb. 2, 1958.
Flüchtlingsgespräche 1961.

POETRY COLLECTIONS

Hauspostille, 1927. *Manual of Piety*, 1966.
Svendburger Gedichte, 1939.
Hundert Gedichte, 1951, 1958.
Gedichte, 1955; *transl.* in *Selected Poems*, 1947.
Gedichte, 7 vols., 1961–.

ESSAYS

Kleines Organon für das Theater in *Versuche*, 12, 1949–57. *Little Organon for the Theatre* in *Accent*, Winter 1951.
Theaterarbeit, 1952; *The German Drama, Pre-Hitler*, in *Left Review*, 1936.
Arendt, Hannah, "What Is Permitted to Jove," in *The New Yorker*, November 5, 1966.
Bentley, Eric, "From Strindberg to Bertolt Brecht" in *The Playwright as Thinker*, 1946.

——————"Introduction" to *Seven Plays by Bertolt Brecht*, New York: Grove Press, Inc.

Demetz, Peter B., editor. *Brecht: A Collection of Critical Essays*, Englewood Cliffs: Prentice-Hall, 1962.

Esslin, Martin. *Brecht: The Man and His Work*. New York: Doubleday & Company, Inc., 1960.

Frisch, Max. "Recollections of Brecht," *The Tulane Drama Review*, vol. 6, 1961.

Gray, Ronald. *Bertolt Brecht*, New York: Grove Press, Inc. 1961.

Grimm, Reinhold. *Bertolt Brecht: Die Struktur seines Werkes*. Nuremberg: Carl Verlag, 1959.

——————*Bertolt Brecht*. Stuttgart: Metzlersche Verlagsbuchhandlung, 1961.

Hays, H.R. "The Poetry of Bertolt Brecht," *Poetry*, vol. 67, 1945.

Kern, Edith. "Brecht's Popular Theatre and Its American Popularity," in *Modern Drama* I December 1958.

——————"Brecht's Epic Theatre and the French Stage," in *Symposium*, Spring 1962.

Lüthy, Herbert, "Of Poor Brecht," *Encounter*, vol. 34, 1956.

Sartre, Jean-Paul. "Brecht et les classiques," in *World Theatre*, vol. VII, 1958.

Tynan, Kenneth. "The Theatre Abroad: Germany", in *The New Yorker*, Sept. 12, 1959.

Weisstein, Ulrich, "Brecht in America: A Preliminary Survey," in *Modern Language Notes*, vol. 78, 1963.

Willett, John, *The Theatre of Bertolt Brecht*, New York: New Directions, 1959.

——————ed. and trans., *Brecht on Theatre: The Development of an Aesthetic*, New York: Hill & Wang 1964.